Inhalt

Hallo!
1.1 Wie geht's? 4
1.2 Wie heißt du? 5
1.3 Wie alt bist du? 6
1.4 Wann hast du Geburtstag? 7
1.5 Mein Klassenzimmer 8
Grammatik 1 9
Grammatik 2 10
Vokabular 11
Kannst du …? Checklist 12

Meine Familie
2.1 Haustiere 13
2.2 Hast du ein Haustier? 14
2.3 Wie ist deine Familie? 15
2.4 Wie bist du? 16
2.5 Brieffreunde 17
Grammatik 1 18
Grammatik 2 19
Vokabular 20
Kannst du …? Checklist 21

Meine Schule
3.1 Meine Schulsachen 22
3.2 Schulfächer 23
3.3 Wie spat ist es? 24
3.4 Mein Schultag 25
3.5 Verben im Präsens 26
Grammatik 1 27
Grammatik 2 28
Vokabular 29
Kannst du …? Checklist 30

Zu Hause
4.1 Meine Adresse 31
4.2 Mein Haus 32
4.3 Und das ist die Küche … 33
4.4 Mein Zimmer 34
Grammatik 1 35
Grammatik 2 36
Vokabular 37
Kannst du …? Checklist 38

Guten Appetit!
5.1 Etwas zum Essen 39
5.2 Mahlzeit! 40
5.3 Ich esse kein Fleisch! 41

5.4 Koch mit!
Grammatik
Grammatik
Vokabular 45
Kannst du …? Checklist 46

Meine Interessen
6.1 Was spielst du gern? 47
6.2 Hobbys 48
6.3 Ich sehe gern fern! 49
6.4 Wie oft machst du …? 50
Grammatik 1 51
Grammatik 2 52
Vokabular 53
Kannst du …? Checklist 54

Meine Stadt
7.1 Woher kommst du? 55
7.2 Willkommen in Hollfeld 56
7.3 Wir fahren nach Bayreuth! 57
7.4 Wie fährst du in die Stadt? 58
Grammatik 1 59
Grammatik 2 60
Vokabular 61
Kannst du …? Checklist 62

Meine Freizeit
8.1 Wie ist das Wetter? 63
8.2 Was machen wir? 64
8.3 Im Supermarkt 65
8.4 Im Café 66
Grammatik 1 67
Grammatik 2 68
Vokabular 69
Kannst du …? Checklist 70

Ein Wochenende in Hollfeld
9.1 Heute Abend fahre ich in die Stadt! 71
9.2 Was machst du am Wochenende? 72
9.3 Was hast du am Samstag gemacht? 73
9.4 Sonntag im Park 74
Grammatik 1 75
Grammatik 2 76
Vokabular 77
Kannst du …? Checklist 78

Meine neuen Wörter 79

drei **3**

1.1 Wie geht's?

Hallo!

1 Schreib Antworten.
Write answers for the greetings.

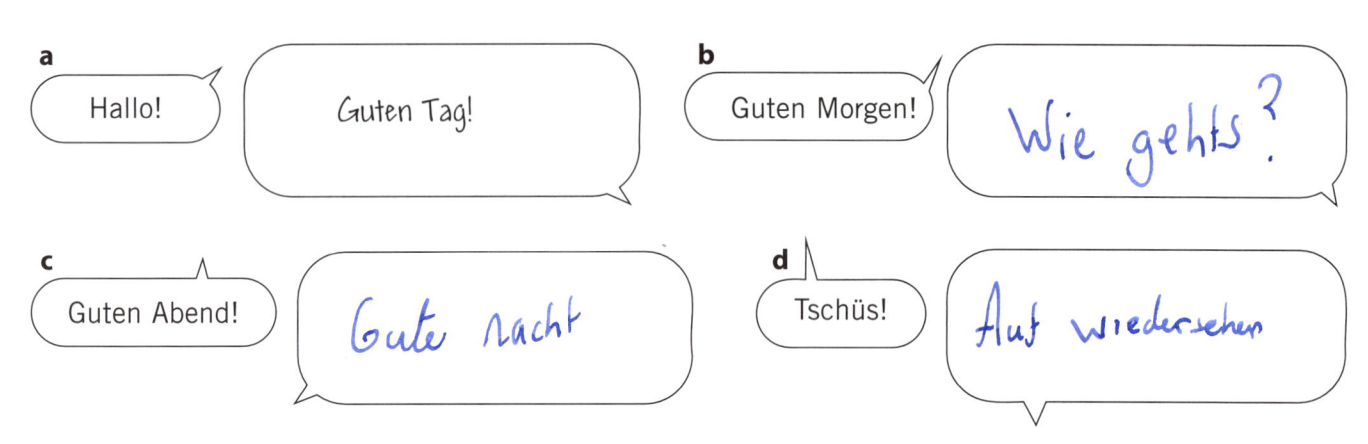

a) Hallo! — Guten Tag!
b) Guten Morgen! — Wie gehts?
c) Guten Abend! — Gute nacht
d) Tschüs! — Auf wiedersehen

2 Wie geht's? Füll die Lücken aus.
Fill in the gaps for each picture.

- Eva: Sehr gut, danke!
- Andi: P_r_i_m_a!
- Tom: S_c_h_l_e_c_h_t!
- Lars: D_a_n_k_e, g_u_t!
- Ina: N_i_c_h_t so g_u_t!

4 vier

1.2 Wie heißt du?

Hallo!

1 Was sagen sie? Füll die Lücken aus.
What are they saying? Fill in the gaps.

A Guten Tag! B _____

A Wie heißt du? B _____

A Wie schreibt man das? B _____

A Danke. Auf Wiedersehen! B _____

Ich heiße Stefan.
Hallo!
Tschüß!
S – T – E – F – A – N.

2 Du bist dran – schreib einen neuen Dialog.
Write a new dialogue like the one in activity 1.

A _____ B _____

A _____ B _____

A _____ B _____

A _____ B _____

fünf 5

1.3 Wie alt bist du?

Hallo!

1 Kreuzworträtsel – schreib die Zahlwörter auf.
Write the numbers in the grid.

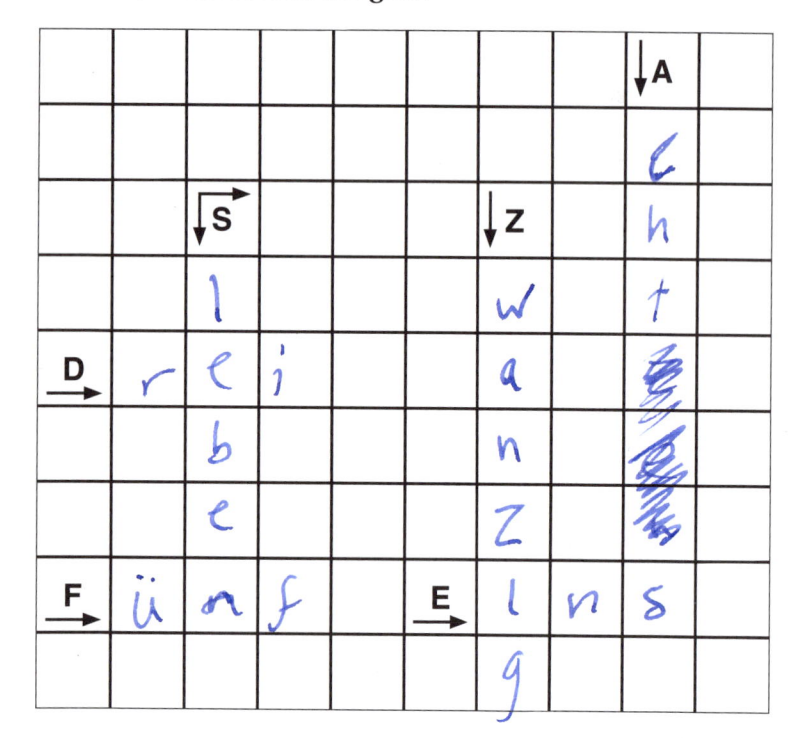

| 16 | 8 | 7 | 3 | 20 | 5 | 1 |

Grid entries (handwritten):
- A (down): s, h, t, (scribbled)
- S (down): l, e, b, e
- Z (down): w, a, n, z
- D (across): r e i
- F (across): ü n f
- E (across): l n s
- (bottom): g

2 Schreib die Zahlen auf.
Write down the numbers.

12 Zwölf   2 Zwei   7 Sieben
15 fünfzehn   6 Sechs   3 drei
4 ~~drei~~ vier   20 Zwanzig   17 Subzehn

3 Schreib die Zahlen auf.
Do the sums.

a vier + elf = fün zehn
b acht + sechs = vierzehn
c neun + drei = elf
d sieben + zwei = neun
e fünf + elf = Sech~~zen~~ zehn
f zehn + eins = elf

6 sechs

1.4 Wann hast du Geburtstag? — Hallo!

1 Was passt? Schreib die passenden Wörter auf.
Write down the months for the seasons.

Frühling: März, April, Mai

Sommer: Juni, Juli, August

Herbst: September, Oktober, November

Winter: December, Januar, Februar

2 Du bist dran – schreib Antworten für die Fragen.
Write your own answers for the questions.

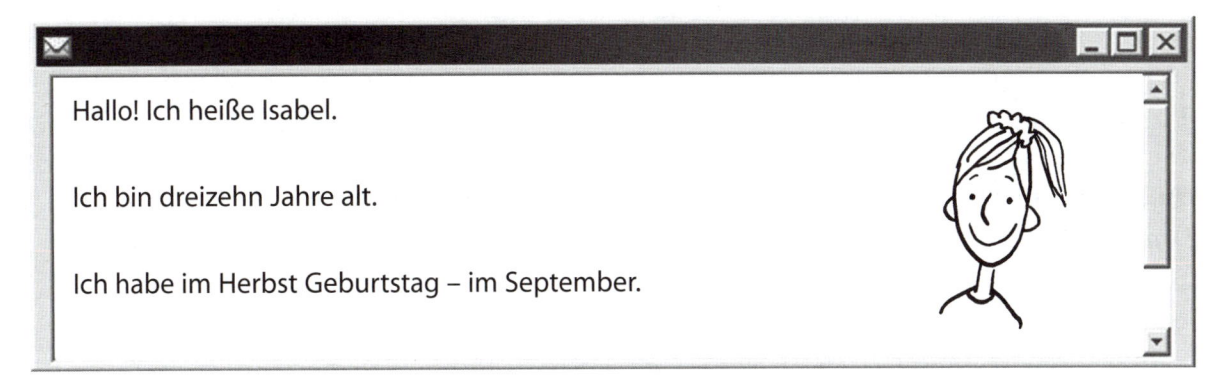

> Hallo! Ich heiße Isabel.
>
> Ich bin dreizehn Jahre alt.
>
> Ich habe im Herbst Geburtstag – im September.

a Wie heißt du?
b Wie alt bist du?
c Wann hast du Geburtstag?

a Ich heiße Ben
b Ich bin dreizehn jahre alt
c ich habe im herbst Geburtstag – im April

sieben 7

1.5 Mein Klassenzimmer

Hallo!

1 Was ist das? Schreib die Wörter auf.
Write down the words for a–h.

a ein Lehrer
b _____
c _____
d _____
e _____
f _____
g _____
h _____

2 Du bist dran! Zeichne dein Klassenzimmer und schreib die Wörter mit *der/die/das* auf.
Draw your classroom and write the words with der/die/das.

8 *acht*

Grammatik 1

Hallo!

1 Schreib die passenden Verben auf.
Write the correct verb for each sentence.

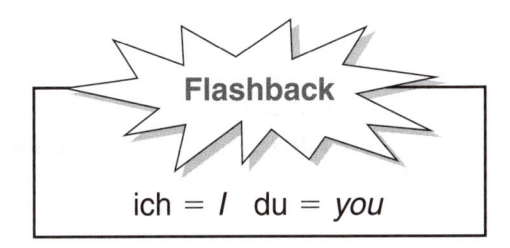

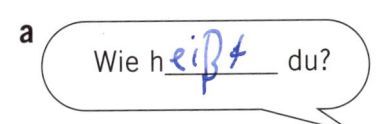

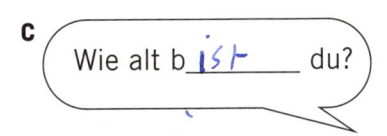

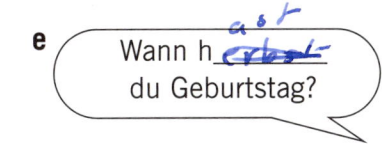

Flashback

ich = I   du = you

a) Wie h_eißt_ du?

b) Ich h_eiße_ Markus.

c) Wie alt b_ist_ du?

d) Ich b_in_ 14 Jahre alt.

e) Wann h~~erbst~~ *ast* du Geburtstag?

f) Ich h_erbst_ im Juni Geburtstag.

2 Lies die Verben und schreib die *ich*- und *du*-Formen auf. Schreib sie dann auf Englisch auf.
Read the new verbs below and write down the correct ich *and* du *forms. Then write them down in English.*

Beispiel:

ich	Englisch	du	Englisch
finde	I find	findest	you find

~~finden~~
trinken
sagen
lernen
schreiben

neun 9

1 Grammatik 2

Hallo!

> **Flashback**
>
> | | | | |
> |---|---|---|---|
> | **Maskulinum** | der/ein Schüler | = | *the/a male pupil* |
> | **Femininum** | die/eine Lehrerin | = | *the/a female teacher* |
> | **Neutrum** | das/ein Klassenzimmer | = | *the/a classroom* |

1 Unterstreiche alle Maskulin-Wörter in Blau, alle Feminin-Wörter in Rot und alle Neutrum-Wörter in Grün.
Underline all masculine words in blue, feminine words in red and all neuter words in green.

a Stuhl   b Tafel   c Fenster   d Schülerin

e Lehrer   f Klassenzimmer   g Schreibtisch   h Tür

2 Schreib die Wörter in Übung 1 mit *der/die/das* auf.
Write down the words in activity 1 with der/die/das.

a _____   b _____

c _____   d _____

e _____   f _____

g _____   h _____

3 Schreib die Wörter mit *der/die/das* oder *ein/eine/ein* auf.
Write the words with der/die/das or ein/eine/ein.

a der Bus _____   b eine Party _____

c eine Bäckerei _____   d das Baby _____

e ein Radio _____   f der Fußball _____

10 *zehn*

1 Vokabular

Hallo!

Guten Tag sagen

Hallo!
Guten Morgen!
Guten Tag!
Guten Abend!
Gute Nacht!
Tschüs!
Auf Wiedersehen!
Wie geht's?
Danke, sehr gut.
Prima.
Gut.
Nicht so gut.
Schlecht.
Wie heißt du?
Ich heiße Melanie.

Geburtstage

Wie alt bist du?
Ich bin 13 Jahre alt.
eins
zwei
drei
vier
fünf
sechs
sieben
acht
neun
zehn
elf
zwölf
dreizehn
vierzehn
fünfzehn
sechzehn
siebzehn
achtzehn
neunzehn
zwanzig

Greetings

Hello!
Good morning!
Good day!
Good evening!
Good night!
Bye!
Goodbye!
How are you?
Very well, thanks.
Great.
Fine.
Not so good.
Awful/Not very well.
What's your name?
I am called Melanie.

Birthdays

How old are you?
I am thirteen years old.
1
2
3
4
5
6
7
8
9
10
11
12
13
14
15
16
17
18
19
20

Wann hast du Geburtstag?
Im Frühling.
Im Sommer.
Im Herbst.
Im Winter.
Ich habe im Januar Geburtstag.
Januar
Februar
März
April
Mai
Juni
Juli
August
September
Oktober
November
Dezember

Meine Klasse/ Schulsachen

Wer ist das?
Das ist der/ein Lehrer.

Das ist die/eine Lehrerin.
Das ist der/ein Schüler.
Das ist die/eine Schülerin.
Was ist das?
Das ist …
der/ein Schreibtisch
der/ein Stuhl
die/eine Tafel
die/eine Tür
die/eine Wand
das/ein Klassenzimmer
das/ein Fenster

When is your birthday?
In the spring.
In the summer.
In the autumn.
In the winter.
My birthday is in January.
January
February
March
April
May
June
July
August
September
October
November
December

My class/Classroom objects

Who's that?
That's the/a teacher (male).
That's the/a teacher (female).
That's the/a pupil (male).
That's the/a pupil (female).
What's that?
That's …
the/a desk
the/a chair
the/a blackboard
the/a door
the/a wall
the/a classroom
the/a window

Kannst du …? Checklist

Hallo!

This is a checklist of the things you should aim to learn in German using Klasse! neu 1. Use the **Check** boxes and the **Prove it!** column to keep track of what you have learned.

★ Tick the first box when you feel you are getting to grips with the learning objective, but sometimes need a prompt or time to think.

★ Tick the second box when you think you have fully mastered the learning objective and will be able to use it again in future.

★ Make notes following the prompts in the **Prove it!** column to help you show what you have learned. Your learning partner or parent can test you and initial the second box to confirm the progress you have made.

Learning objectives	Check	Prove it!
I can say 'Hello', 'Goodbye' and 'How are you?'	☐ ☐	*Get partner to test you.*
I can introduce myself.	☐ ☐	*Get partner to test you.*
I can ask someone his/her name.	☐ ☐	*Get partner to test you.*
I can recite the German alphabet.	☐ ☐	*Get partner to test you.*
I can count to 20.	☐ ☐	*Get partner to test you.*
I can say and write the names of the months.	☐ ☐	*Write them down without looking at your book.*
I can say and write the names of the seasons.	☐ ☐	*Write them down without looking at your book.*
I can give my age.	☐ ☐	*Get partner to test you.*
I can ask someone his/her age.	☐ ☐	*Get partner to test you.*
I can say when my birthday is.	☐ ☐	*Get partner to test you.*
I can ask when someone's birthday is.	☐ ☐	*Get partner to test you.*
I can describe my classroom.	☐ ☐	*Get partner to test you.*
I know it's important to learn the gender of a noun at the same time as the spelling and pronunciation.	☐ ☐	*Explain why to a partner.*
I know the gender of some common nouns.	☐ ☐	*Without looking at your book, write der/die/das for:* Lehrer, Schülerin, Klassenzimmer, Stuhl, Tafel.
I can form simple questions.	☐ ☐	*Without looking at your book, write questions using:* wie, wann, wer, was.
I can recognize words for 'a' and 'the'.	☐ ☐	*Get partner to test you.*
I can recognize the different sounds *ei* and *ie*.	☐ ☐	*Read aloud:* ein, wie, drei, sieben, zwei, vier.
I can greet people appropriately.	☐ ☐	*Get partner to test you.*
I can find six places on a map of Germany, Austria and Switzerland.	☐ ☐	*Show a partner where to look.*

2.1 Haustiere

Meine Familie

1 Wie schreibt man diese Haustiere?
What are the names of these animals in German?

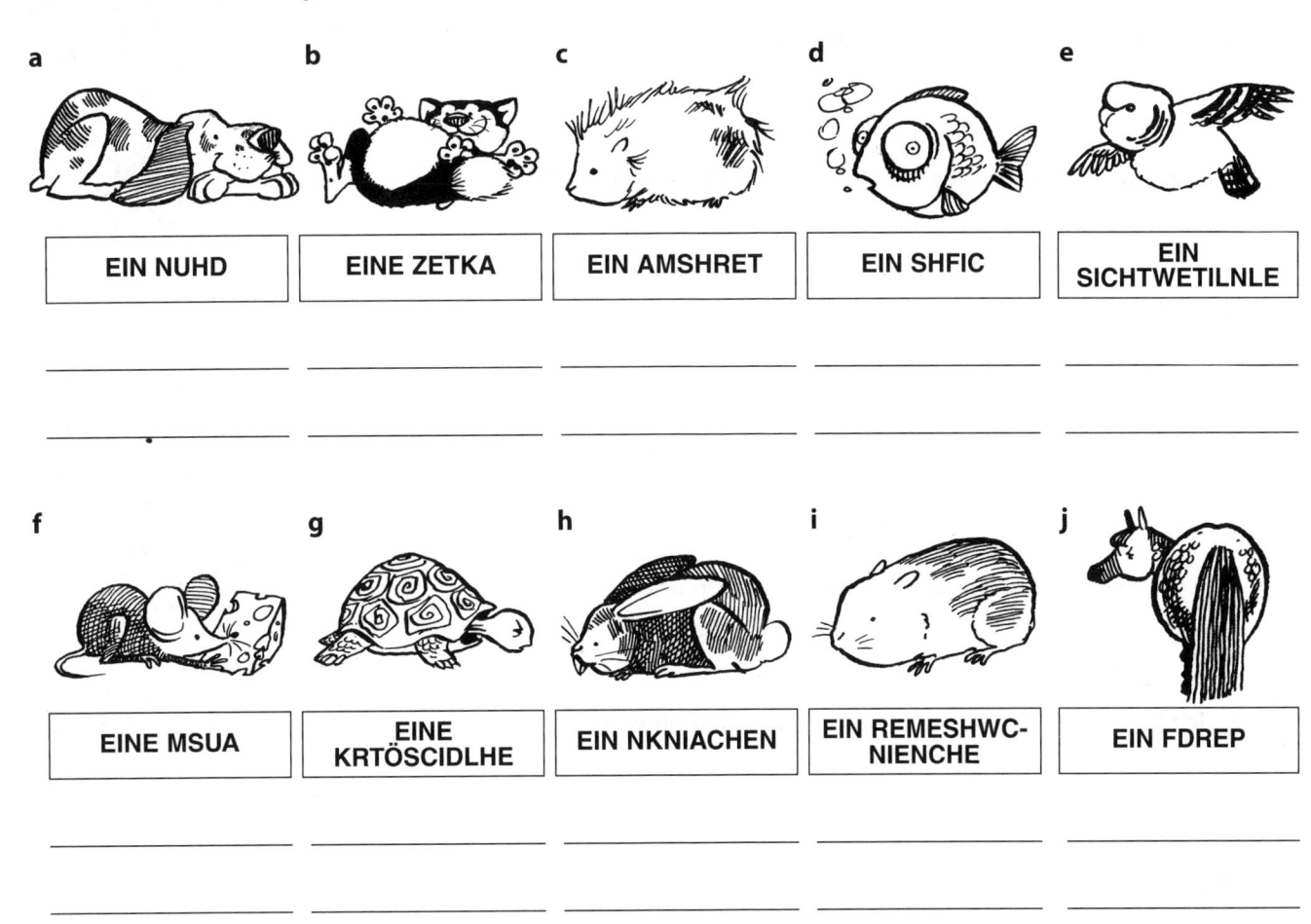

a | EIN NUHD
b | EINE ZETKA
c | EIN AMSHRET
d | EIN SHFIC
e | EIN SICHTWETILNLE

f | EINE MSUA
g | EINE KRTÖSCIDLHE
h | EIN NKNIACHEN
i | EIN REMESHWC-NIENCHE
j | EIN FDREP

2 *ein* oder *eine*? Füll die Lücken aus.
ein or eine? Fill in the blanks.

a _____ Pferd
b _____ Maus
c _____ Katze
d _____ Hund

e _____ Wellensittich
f _____ Hamster
g _____ Schildkröte
h _____ Kaninchen

3 Was passt zusammen?
Draw lines to match up the sentences.

1 Das ist ein Hund.
2 Das ist eine Schildkröte.
3 Das ist ein Pferd.

a Es ist braun.
b Er ist schwarz.
c Sie ist grün.

dreizehn 13

2.2 # Hast du ein Haustier? *Meine Familie*

1 **Was passt zusammen?**
Draw lines to match up the sentences and pictures.

1 Ich habe drei Fische, zwei Katzen und einen Hund.   a

2 Ich habe zwei Meerschweinchen, drei Mäuse und ein Pferd.   b

3 Ich habe einen Wellensittich, zwei Kaninchen und einen Hund.   c

4 Ich habe zwei Katzen, drei Hamster und eine Maus.   d

5 Ich habe zwei Katzen, drei Meerschweinchen und ein Pferd.   e

6 Ich habe zwei Fische, einen Wellensittich und einen Hund.   f

2 **Was sagt Uli?**
What does Uli say?

zwei Katzen   einen Wellensittich
vier Hunde   ein Pferd   einen Fisch
vier Fische   drei Meerschweinchen
drei Katzen   zwei Hunde
zwei Meerschweinchen
zwei Schildkröten

Ich habe …

14   *vierzehn*

2.3 Wie ist deine Familie? — *Meine Familie*

1 Worträtsel. Finde die Personen.
Find the family members in the word search.

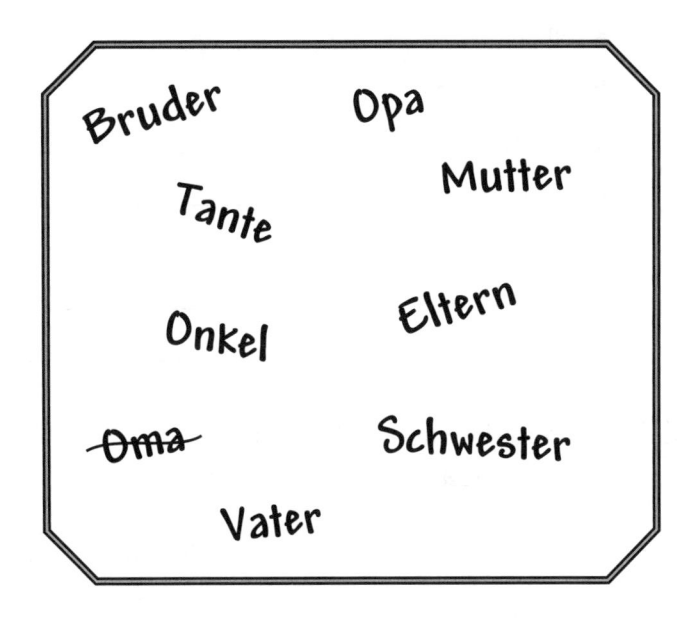

T	O	M	R	K	B	O	P	A	U
A	O	S	O	M	A	N	V	R	J
N	V	C	F	L	S	K	A	A	U
T	A	H	R	C	M	E	T	E	B
E	T	W	E	M	U	L	H	P	R
R	E	E	L	W	T	B	V	V	U
O	R	S	T	L	L	B	N	A	D
B	A	T	E	O	E	S	V	T	E
E	M	E	R	M	U	T	T	E	R
L	X	R	N	K	E	H	D	U	M

Bruder   Opa
Tante   Mutter
Onkel   Eltern
~~Oma~~   Schwester
Vater

2 Füll die Lücken aus.
Fill in the gaps to describe Karl's family.

_____Meine Mutter_____ heißt Maria.
_____ heißt Ilse.
_____ heißt Jochen.
_____ heißt Sara.
_____ heißt Thomas.
_____ heißt Gisela.
_____ heißt Albrecht.
_____ heißt Stefan.
_____ heißt Anne.
_____ heißt David.

Ich heiße Karl.

Gisela — Albrecht
Maria — Thomas   Sara — Jochen
Karl   Ilse   Stefan   Anne   David

fünfzehn 15

2.4 Wie bist du?

Meine Familie

1 Finde die Adjektive.
Find the adjectives.

a NUJG _____
b NELILTETGNI _____
c NRETS _____
d ELKNI _____
e EDCRILHNUF _____
f ERFHC _____
g FELIßGI _____

h TAL _____
i TUAL _____
j AFLU _____
k ELSEI _____
l RGOß _____
m SRLTCIHPO _____
n SKUIIASLHCM _____

2 Schreib die Sätze richtig auf.
Write the sentences out correctly.

a [Carl] [Er] [heißt] [.] [Er] [und] [ist] [groß] [freundlich] [.]

Er heißt Carl. _____

b [Schwester] [Martina] [heißt] [Meine] [.] [Sie] [jung] [ist] [und] [klein] [.]

_____

c [Mein] [ist] [musikalisch] [Vater] [.] [sehr] [ist] [fleißig] [Er] [.]

_____

d [nicht] [sind] [gar] [Eltern] [faul] [Meine] [.] [sportlich] [Sie] [sehr] [sind] [.]

_____

3 Du bist dran! Beschreib drei Personen in deiner Familie.
Describe three people in your family.

Beispiel: Mein Bruder ist sehr freundlich, aber gar nicht alt. Er ist nicht sportlich, aber sehr fleißig. Er ist sehr laut und ziemlich klein.

1 _____

2 _____

3 _____

16 sechzehn

2.5 Brieffreunde

Meine Familie

1 Welche Fragen und Antworten passen zusammen?
Draw lines to match up the questions and answers.

1 Wann hast du Geburtstag?   a Ich heiße Monika.
2 Hast du Haustiere?   b Im Winter.
3 Wie heißt du?   c Sie ist sportlich und intelligent.
4 Wie heißt dein Vater?   d Er ist 18 Jahre alt.
5 Wie ist deine Mutter?   e Sie ist 14 Jahre alt.
6 Wie alt ist deine Schwester?   f Er heißt Alf.
7 Wie alt ist dein Bruder?   g Ja, ich habe ein Kaninchen.

2 Füll die Lücken im Text aus.
Fill in the gaps.

> sie   bin   ist   heiße
> sportlich   habe   nicht
> ziemlich   auch

Ich _____ Max und ich _____ 13 Jahre alt. Ich _____ im April Geburtstag. Ich habe eine Schwester, _____ heißt Tanja und sie _____ 12 Jahre alt. Sie ist _____ intelligent und auch sehr _____ .

Ich habe _____ eine Katze. Sie ist alt und _____ sehr freundlich.

3 Beschreib vier Personen mit den folgenden Vokabeln.
Write sentences to describe four people using the following words.

> sehr   ziemlich   nicht   auch   und   aber

_____
_____
_____
_____
_____
_____

siebzehn **17**

Grammatik 1

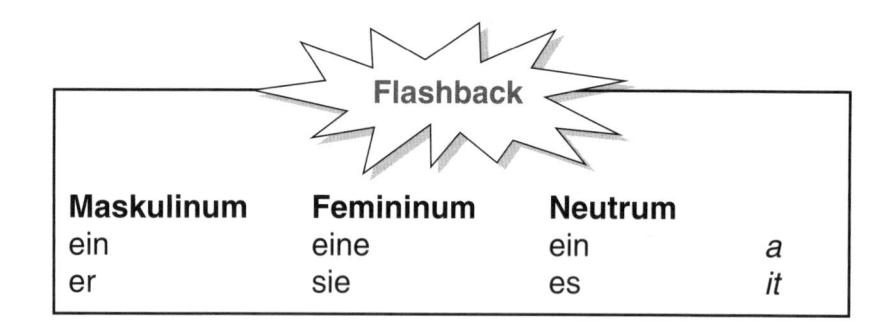

Meine Familie

Flashback

Maskulinum	Femininum	Neutrum	
ein	eine	ein	*a*
er	sie	es	*it*

1 Füll die Lücken mit *ein* oder *eine* und *er*, *sie* oder *es* aus.
Fill in the gaps with ein *or* eine *and* er, sie *or* es.

a Das ist _____ Hund. _____ ist braun.
b Das ist _____ Schildkröte. _____ ist grün.
c Das ist _____ Pferd. _____ ist schwarz.
d Das ist _____ Katze. _____ ist braun und weiß.
e Das ist _____ Meerschweinchen. _____ ist klein.
f Das ist _____ Fisch. _____ ist rot und blau.

2 Beschreib die Bilder.
Write down what the pictures show you.

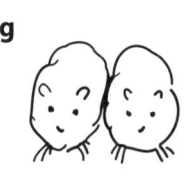

Flashback

To make most English nouns plural, you add an -s.
German nouns form their plurals in different ways:

eine Katze → zwei Katze**n**
ein Fisch → zwei Fisch**e**
eine Maus → zwei M**äu**s**e**
ein Meerschweinchen → zwei Meerschweinchen

a _____
b _____
c _____
d _____
e _____
f _____
g _____

18 *achtzehn*

2 Grammatik 2

Meine Familie

Flashback

Remember the different endings and verb forms:

ich	bin	habe	heiße
du	bist	hast	heißt
er/sie/es	ist	hat	heißt

1 Füll die Lücken aus.
Fill in the gaps.

a Meine Schwester _____ im Juli Geburtstag.
b Mein Hund _____ Max.
c Wann _____ du Geburtstag?
d Mein Bruder _____ 14 Jahre alt.
e Wie alt _____ du?
f Ich _____ im Juni Geburtstag.
g Ich _____ 12 Jahre alt.

2 Übersetze ins Deutsche.
Translate into German.

a I have a guinea pig. _____
b It is small and white. _____
c My sister is called Elsa. _____
d Her birthday is in May. _____
e My father is 44 years old. _____
f My mother is quiet and friendly. _____

3 Schreib Sätze mit diesen Vokabeln.
Use the words on the wall to make up sentences. Use as many words as you can.

| ich | sehr | ist | nicht | bin | hat |
| er | sie | ziemlich | habe | es | bin |

_____
_____

neunzehn 19

Vokabular

Meine Familie

Haustiere — *Pets*

Das ist ... — *That is ...*
ein Hund — *a dog*
ene Katze — *a cat*
ein Fisch — *a fish*
ein Wellensittich — *a budgie*
eine Schildkröte — *a tortoise*
ein Pferd — *a horse*
ein Hamster — *a hamster*
ein Meerschweinchen — *a guinea pig*
ein Kaninchen — *a rabbit*
eine Maus — *a mouse*
Er/sie/es ist ... — *It is ...*
blau — *blue*
braun — *brown*
rot — *red*
grün — *green*
gelb — *yellow*
schwarz — *black*
weiß — *white*
orange — *orange*
grau — *grey*

Hast du ein Haustier? — *Have you got a pet?*

Ich habe ... — *I have ...*
  einen Hund — *a dog*
  eine Katze — *a cat*
  ein Meerschweinchen — *a guinea pig*
  zwei Pferde — *two horses*
  zwei Schildkröten — *two tortoises*
  zwei Mäuse — *two mice*
Ich habe keine Haustiere. — *I don't have any pets.*

Wie ist deine Familie? — *What's your family like?*

Hast du Geschwister? — *Do you have brothers and sisters?*
Ich habe ... — *I have ...*
  einen Bruder/eine Schwester — *a brother/a sister*
  einen Halbbruder/eine Halbschwester — *a half-brother/a half-sister*
  einen Stiefbruder/eine Stiefschwester — *a stepbrother/a stepsister*
  zwei Brüder/zwei Schwestern — *two brothers/two sisters*
Ich habe keine Geschwister. — *I have no brothers and sisters.*
Ich bin Einzelkind. — *I am an only child.*
Das ist ... — *That is ...*
mein Bruder/mein Halbbruder — *my brother/my half-brother*
meine Schwester/meine Halbschwester — *my sister/my half-sister*
mein Vater/mein Stiefvater — *my father/my stepfather*
meine Mutter/meine Stiefmutter — *my mother/my stepmother*
mein Onkel — *my uncle*
meine Tante — *my aunt*
mein Großvater — *my grandfather*
meine Großmutter — *my grandmother*
mein Cousin — *my cousin (m.)*
meine Cousine — *my cousin (f.)*
Wie heißt dein Vater/deine Mutter? — *What is your father/mother called?*

Wie bist du? — *What are you like?*

musikalisch — *musical*
fleißig — *hard-working*
jung — *young*
freundlich — *friendly*
frech — *cheeky*
alt — *old*
ernst — *serious*
groß — *tall*
faul — *lazy*
leise — *quiet*
intelligent — *intelligent*
sportlich — *sporty*
klein — *small*
laut — *loud*
sehr — *very*
ziemlich — *quite*
nicht — *not*
gar nicht — *not at all*
Wie ist dein Bruder/deine Schwester? — *What is your brother/your sister like?*

20   *zwanzig*

2 Kannst du ...? Checklist

Meine Familie

This is a checklist of the things you should aim to learn in German using Klasse! neu 1. *Use the* **Check** *boxes and the* **Prove it!** *column to keep track of what you have learned.*

★ Tick the first box when you feel you are getting to grips with the learning objective, but sometimes need a prompt or time to think.

★ Tick the second box when you think you have fully mastered the learning objective and will be able to use it again in future.

★ Make notes following the prompts in the **Prove it!** column to help you show what you have learned. Your learning partner or parent can test you and initial the second box to confirm the progress you have made.

Learning objectives	Check	Prove it!
I can say whether I have pets.	☐ ☐	*Get partner to test you.*
I can ask someone whether he/she has any pets.	☐ ☐	*Get partner to test you.*
I can say and write the names of eight pets.	☐ ☐	*Write them down and say aloud to a partner.*
I can say what colour pets are.	☐ ☐	*Get partner to test you.*
I can say and write the names of family members.	☐ ☐	*Write them down and say aloud to a partner.*
I can describe myself and members of my family.	☐ ☐	*Get partner to test you.*
I can ask someone if he/she has any brothers and sisters.	☐ ☐	*Get partner to test you.*
I can say if I have any brothers and sisters.	☐ ☐	*Get partner to test you.*
I can ask what somebody's name is.	☐ ☐	*Get partner to test you.*
I can give two different words for 'my' and explain why there are two.	☐ ☐	*Get partner to test you.*
I can use *einen/eine/ein* and *keinen/keine/kein* correctly after *ich habe* ...	☐ ☐	*Get partner to test you.*
I can write a longer description.	☐ ☐	*Get partner to test you.*
I know some high-frequency words and understand their importance.	☐ ☐	*Choose which three of the following are high-frequency, give their meaning and use them in a sentence:* sehr, alt, und, Katze, aber, Bruder.

einundzwanzig **21**

3.1 Meine Schulsachen

Meine Schule

1 Was hast du? Schreib die passenden Wörter auf. Schreib auch *ein* oder *eine* auf.
Write the correct words for the pictures with ein or eine.

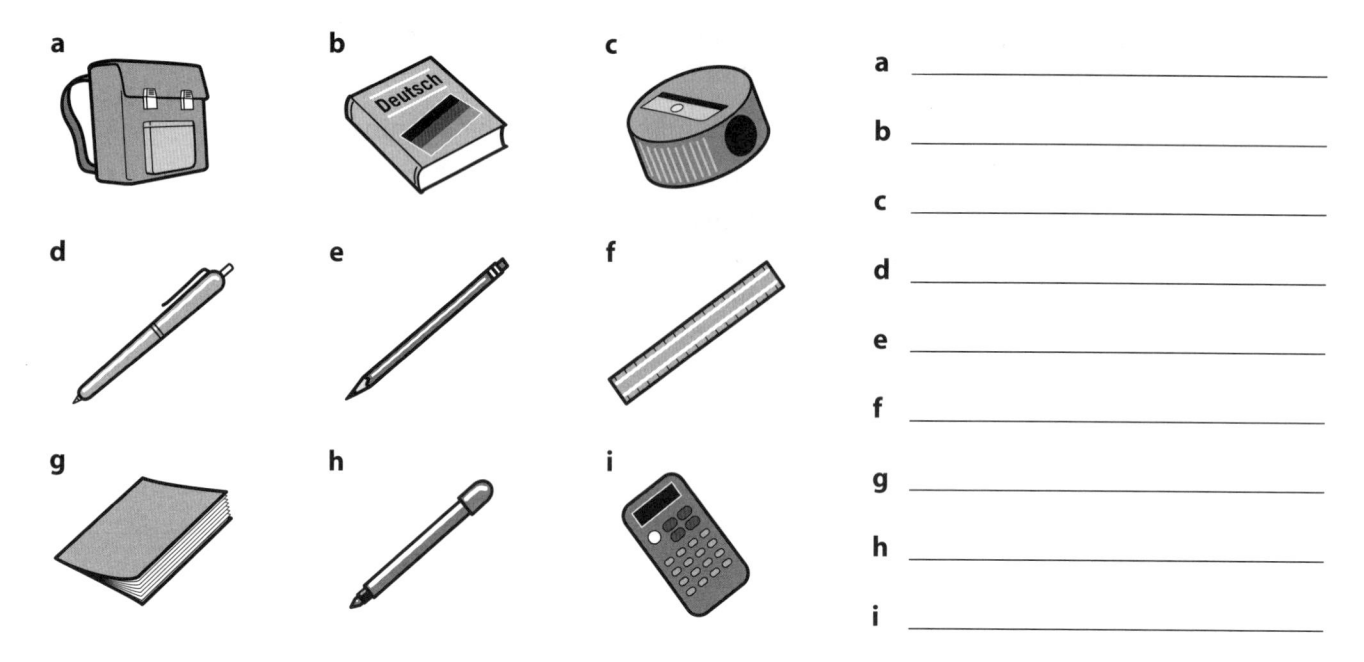

a   _____

b   _____

c   _____

d   _____

e   _____

f   _____

g   _____

h   _____

i   _____

2 Unterstreiche die passenden Wörter.
Underline the correct article for each sentence.

a Ich habe eine/einen Kuli.
b Hast du ein/eine Heft?
c Ich habe ein/eine Tasche.
d Ich habe einen/eine Bleistift.
e Hast du ein/einen Anspitzer?
f Ich habe einen/ein Buch.

3 Du bist dran! Zeichne deine Tasche. Was hast du? Schreib Sätze.
Draw and describe your schoolbag.

Beispiel: Ich habe einen Kuli.

22 *zweiundzwanzig*

3.2 Schulfächer

Meine Schule

1 Schreib die passenden Schulfächer auf.
Write down the school subjects.

a _____ b _____ c _____ d _____ e _____

f _____ g _____ h _____ i _____ j _____

2 „Wie findest du…?" Schreib Sätze.
Write sentences.

♡ = prima
interessant
super
fantastisch

✗ = langweilig
schwer
doof
furchtbar

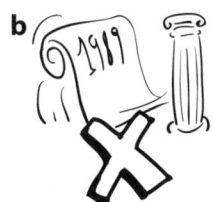

Beispiel:

a Ich finde Deutsch prima.

b _____

c _____

d _____

e _____

f _____

3.3 Wie spät ist es?

Meine Schule

1 Zeichne die richtigen Uhrzeiten auf.
Draw the correct time on the clocks.

- **a** Es ist Viertel nach elf. 
- **b** Es ist Mittag. 
- **c** Es ist halb vier. 
- **d** Es ist sieben Uhr.

2 Schreib die richtigen Uhrzeiten auf.
Write the correct time.

- **a** Es ist _____
- **b** _____ 
- **c** _____ 
- **d** _____

3 Wie spät ist es? Was hast du? Schreib Sätze.
What subjects do you have when? Write sentences.

- **a**  + 8.45
- **b**  + 9.30
- **c**  + 12.15
- **d** 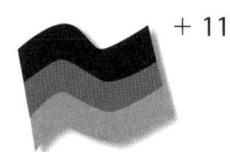 + 11
- **e**  + 13.30
- **f**  + 10.15

- **a** Es ist Viertel vor neun. Ich habe Mathe.
- **b** _____
- **c** _____
- **d** _____
- **e** _____
- **f** _____

24 *vierundzwanzig*

3.4 Mein Schultag

Meine Schule

1a Füll die Lücken aus.
Fill in the gaps.

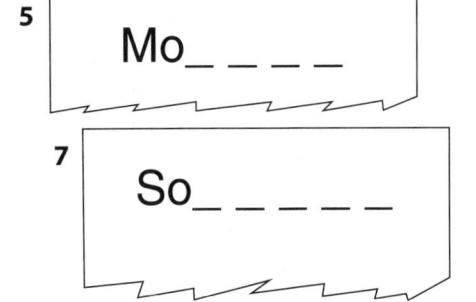

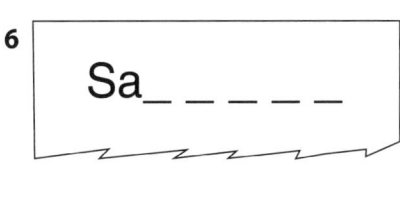

1. Di_ _ _ _ _ _
2. Do_ _ _ _ _ _ _ _
3. Fr_ _ _ _ _
4. Mi_ _ _ _ _ _
5. Mo_ _ _ _
6. Sa_ _ _ _ _
7. So_ _ _ _

1b Schreib die richtige Reihenfolge auf.
Write the days in the correct order.

Montag — Monday

1c Wie heißt das auf Englisch?
Write the English.

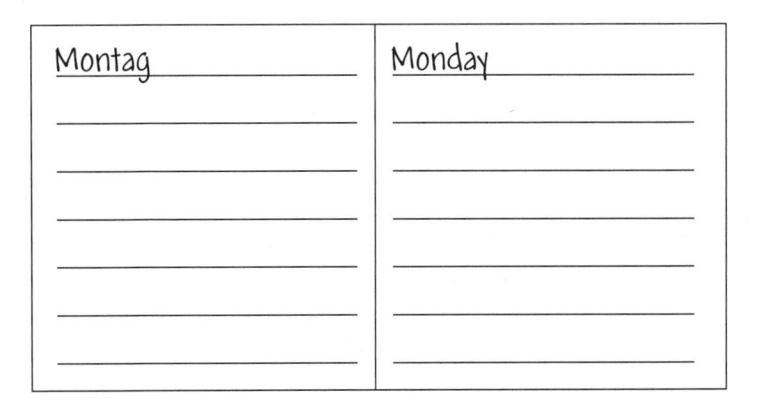

2 Was hast du wann? Schreib Sätze.
Write sentences with the information.

Beispiel:

a Montag: Am Montag um neun Uhr habe ich Mathe.

b Dienstag: _____

c Mittwoch: _____

d Donnerstag: _____

e Freitag: _____

f Samstag: _____

fünfundzwanzig **25**

3.5 Verben im Präsens — *Meine Schule*

Flashback

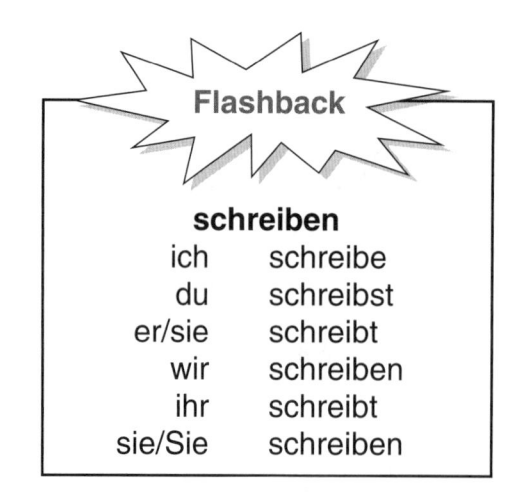

schreiben
ich	schreibe
du	schreibst
er/sie	schreibt
wir	schreiben
ihr	schreibt
sie/Sie	schreiben

1 Schreib die passenden Wörter auf Englisch auf.
Write down the correct pronouns in English.

a ich _____
b du _____
c er _____
d sie (sing.) _____
e wir _____
f ihr _____
g Sie _____
h sie (pl.) _____

2 Füll die Lücken aus.
Fill in the correct verb endings.

a Ich find_____ Deutsch prima.
b Er mach_____ Pause.
c Wie heiß_____ du?
d Ihr hör_____ gut zu.
e Sie schreib_____ eine E-Mail.
f Wie finde_____ du Mathe?
g Wir mach_____ Hausaufgaben.

3 Schreib die Sätze auf Deutsch.
Write the sentences in German.

a What do you think of PE? _____
b She's called Melanie. _____
c Listen carefully! _____
d They are called Tom and Tina. _____
e We are writing a dialogue. _____

26 sechsundzwanzig

Grammatik 1

Meine Schule

1 Schreib *she*, *they* oder *you* für die Sätze.
Write she, they or you under the sentences.

Flashback

sie = *she* + *they*   **Sie** = *you (polite)*

Beispiel:

a  Haben Sie ein Heft?
you

b  Sie ist vierzehn Jahre alt.
____

c  Sie sind sehr klein!
____

d  Wann haben Sie Kunst?
____

e  Sie haben einen Hund.
____

f  Sie ist sehr sportlich!
____

Flashback

Ich habe am Freitag Kunst.   →   Am Freitag habe ich Kunst.

2 Schreib Sätze.
Write sentences with the information.

Beispiel:

a Montag   er   _Am Montag hat er Sport._

b Dienstag   ihr   ____

c Mittwoch   sie (pl.)   ____

d Donnerstag   du   ____

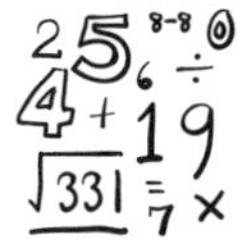

e Freitag   wir   ____

f Samstag   ich   ____

siebenundzwanzig **27**

3 Grammatik 2

Meine Schule

1 Füll die Sätze mit *haben* aus.
Fill in the correct form of the verb haben.

a Wir _____ Englisch.

b Susi _____ kein Heft.

c _____ Sie ein Lineal, Frau May?

d Ich _____ am Montag Sport.

e _____ ihr ein Buch?

f Wann _____ du Naturwissenschaften?

g _____ sie (pl.) am Freitag Musik?

h Er _____ eine Bleistift.

Flashback

haben *to have*
ich habe
du hast
er/sie/es hat
wir haben
ihr habt
sie/Sie haben

2 Füll die Sätze mit *sein* aus.
Fill in the correct form of the verb sein.

a Ich _____ dreizehn Jahre alt.

b Mathe _____ mein Lieblingsfach.

c Das _____ meine Eltern.

d _____ du vierzehn Jahre alt?

e Ihr _____ musikalisch.

f Wir _____ freundlich.

g _____ Sie sportlich?

h Sie (sing.) _____ leise.

Flashback

sein *to be*
ich bin
du bist
er/sie/es ist
wir sind
ihr seid
sie/Sie sind

3 *Haben* oder *sein*? Schreib die richtigen Verben auf.
Haben or sein? *Write the correct verbs.*

a Wir _____ um neun Uhr Deutsch.

b Es _____ halb zwölf.

c _____ du ein Lineal?

d Ich _____ keinen Anspitzer.

e Ihr _____ fünfzehn Jahre alt.

f Wann _____ sie Mathe?

g Sie (sing.) _____ intelligent.

h Er _____ am Dienstag Geschichte.

28 *achtundzwanzig*

3 Vokabular — Meine Schule

Meine Schulsachen

Hast du …?

Haben Sie …?
  einen Bleistift
  einen Filzstift
  einen Füller
  einen Kuli
  einen Rechner
  einen Radiergummi
  einen Anspitzer
  eine Tasche
  ein Buch
  ein Heft
  ein Lineal
Ja, ich habe …
Hier, bitte.
Nein, leider nicht.
Ich habe keinen Kuli.
Ich habe keine Tasche.
Ich habe kein Buch.

Schulfächer

Deutsch
Englisch
Erdkunde
Französisch
Geschichte
Informatik
Kunst
Mathe
Musik
Naturwissenschaften
  (Biologie, Chemie,
   Physik)
Religion
Sport
Was ist dein
  Lieblingsfach?

My classroom objects

Do you have …?
  (informal)
Do you have …? (formal)
  a pencil
  a felt-tip pen
  a fountain pen
  a ballpoint pen
  a calculator
  a rubber
  a pencil sharpener
  a bag
  a book
  an exercise book
  a ruler
Yes, I have …
Here you are.
No, sorry.
I don't have a pen.
I don't have a bag.
I don't have a book.

School subjects

German
English
Geography
French
History
IT
Art
Maths
Music
Science
  (Biology, Chemistry,
   Physics)
Religious Studies
PE
What's your favourite
  subject?

Mein Lieblingsfach ist
  Sport.
Wie findest du Sport?
Sport ist …
  prima/super
  fantastisch/interessant
  furchtbar/langweilig
  doof

Wie spät ist es?

Wie spät ist es?
Es ist …
  zwei Uhr
  halb zwei
  Viertel vor zwei
  Viertel nach zwei
  Mittag
  Mitternacht

Mein Schultag

Wann hast du …?
Wann haben wir …?
Um neun Uhr.
Was hast du am …?
Am … habe ich …
  Montag
  Dienstag
  Mittwoch
  Donnerstag
  Freitag
  Samstag
  Sonntag
Am Samstag habe ich
  frei!
Am Sonntag habe ich
  keine Schule!

My favourite subject is
  PE.
What do you think of PE?
PE is …
  excellent/great
  fantastic/interesting
  awful/boring
  stupid

What time is it?

What time is it?
It is …
  two o'clock
  half past one
  quarter to two
  quarter past two
  noon
  midnight

My school day

When do you have …?
When do we have …?
At nine o'clock.
What do you have on …?
On … I have …
  Monday
  Tuesday
  Wednesday
  Thursday
  Friday
  Saturday
  Sunday
On Saturdays, I'm free!

On Sundays, I don't have
  school!

3   Kannst du …? Checklist   *Meine Schule*

This is a checklist of the things you should aim to learn in German using Klasse! neu 1. *Use the* **Check** *boxes and the* **Prove it!** *column to keep track of what you have learned.*

★ Tick the first box when you feel you are getting to grips with the learning objective, but sometimes need a prompt or time to think.

★ Tick the second box when you think you have fully mastered the learning objective and will be able to use it again in future.

★ Make notes following the prompts in the **Prove it!** column to help you show what you have learned. Your learning partner or parent can test you and initial the second box to confirm the progress you have made.

Learning objectives	Check	Prove it!
I can ask someone what classroom objects he/she has.	☐ ☐	*Get partner to test you.*
I can say what classroom objects I have/don't have.	☐ ☐	*Get partner to test you.*
I can ask for classroom objects from my partner/teacher.	☐ ☐	*Get partner/teacher to test you.*
I can ask someone which school subjects he/she likes.	☐ ☐	*Get partner/teacher to test you.*
I can say which subjects I like and dislike.	☐ ☐	*Get partner to test you.*
I can give opinions.	☐ ☐	*Get partner to test you.*
I can ask and say the time.	☐ ☐	*Get partner to test you.*
I can ask when someone has different subjects.	☐ ☐	*Get partner to test you.*
I can say when I have different subjects.	☐ ☐	*Get partner to test you.*
I can say the days of the week.	☐ ☐	*Get partner to test you.*
I can read a German timetable.	☐ ☐	*Check the timetable on page 43 of the Students' Book again.*
I can use *du, ihr* or *Sie* correctly when I say 'you' to different people.	☐ ☐	*Get partner to test you.*
I know the present tense of *sein*.	☐ ☐	*Get partner to test you.*
I know the present tense of *haben*.	☐ ☐	*Get partner to test you.*
I know the present tense of some weak/regular verbs.	☐ ☐	*How do you say: I find, he finds, Ellen and Max find? Check your answers with a partner.*
I can write a sentence in German where the verb always comes second.	☐ ☐	*Get partner to test you.*
I can use different strategies to learn new words.	☐ ☐	*Tell a partner what you might do to learn new words.*
I know some of the differences between German and British schools.	☐ ☐	*Tell a partner three differences.*

4.1 Meine Adresse — *Zu Hause*

1 Schreib die Zahlen in Wörtern auf.
Write the numbers as words.

a **37**   b **63**   c **82**   d **54**   e **49**   f **98**   g **71**   h **26**

a _____   e _____
b _____   f _____
c _____   g _____
d _____   h _____

2 Wo wohnt Familie Maus? Schreib Sätze.
Where does the Maus family live? Follow the lines and write sentences.

82   17   46   39   55   21   63   78

Milli   Martin   Molli   Maxi   Monika   Melli   Micki   Muschi

Beispiel: Milli wohnt in Nummer neununddreißig.

_____
_____
_____

3 Schreib Sätze.
Write sentences to answer these questions.

Wo wohnst du? _____

Wie ist deine Adresse? _____

einunddreißig 31

4.2 Mein Haus

Zu Hause

1 Was ist das? Schreib die passenden Wörter auf.
What is it? Fill in the correct words.

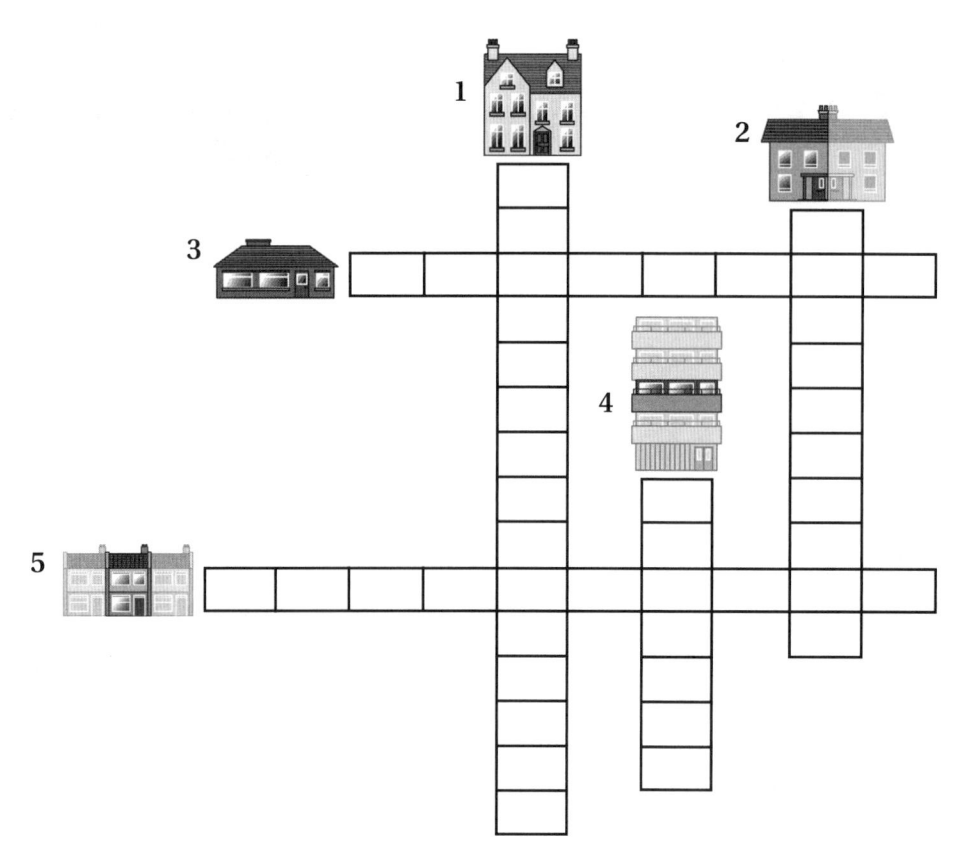

2 Schreib die Sätze zu Ende.
Complete the sentences.

a Tanja wohnt _____

b Olaf wohnt _____

c Wiebke wohnt _____

d Johannes wohnt _____

e Ilka wohnt _____

32 *zweiunddreißig*

4.3 Und das ist die Küche … *Zu Hause*

1 Was gibt es im Haus? Finde die Haus-Wörter.
What is there in the house? Find the vocabulary.

1 ZIMBADEMER — Badezimmer
2 ÜKECH — _____
3 MERESSZIM — _____
4 ZISAFECHLRMM — _____
5 REIMWNZMHO — _____
6 NOLKBA — _____
7 SCDHUE — _____

2 Beschreib das Haus.
Write sentences to describe the house.

Beispiel: Die Küche ist im Erdgeschoss. Sie ist groß und modern.

| groß modern |
| schön klein hässlich |
| unordentlich alt |

dreiunddreißig 33

4.4 Mein Zimmer

Zu Hause

1 Schreib die Wörter auf.
Label the items.

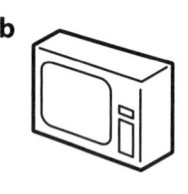

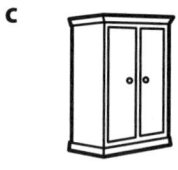

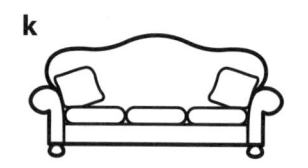

a _____ b _____ c _____ d _____

e _____ f _____ g _____ h _____

i _____ j _____ k _____

2 Beschreib dieses Zimmer. Benutze die Vokabeln im Kasten.
Describe the room. Use the words in the box.

Der Fernseher	ist	dem	dem Tisch.
Die	ist	auf dem	Bett.	ist	ist
auf	ist	Die Kleidung	Stereoanlage	
unter	Regal.	Der Kleiderschrank	
dem Sofa und	dem Sofa.	ist	neben
hinter	Der Schreibtisch	Der	Stuhl
dem Bett.	zwischen	dem Schreibtisch.	

_____
_____
_____
_____

34 vierunddreißig

Grammatik 1

4 — *Zu Hause*

1 Füll die Lücken aus: *einem* oder *einer*?
Fill in the gaps: einem *or* einer?

a Ich wohne in _____ Bungalow.
b Ich wohne in _____ Wohnung.
c Ich wohne in _____ Doppelhaus.
d Ich wohne in _____ Reihenhaus.

Flashback

Ich wohne in **einem** Reihenhaus.
Ich wohne in **einer** Wohnung.

2 Was sagen sie? Schreib Sprechblasen.
What are the people saying? Fill in the speech bubbles.

a Ich wohne in einer Wohnung.
b
c

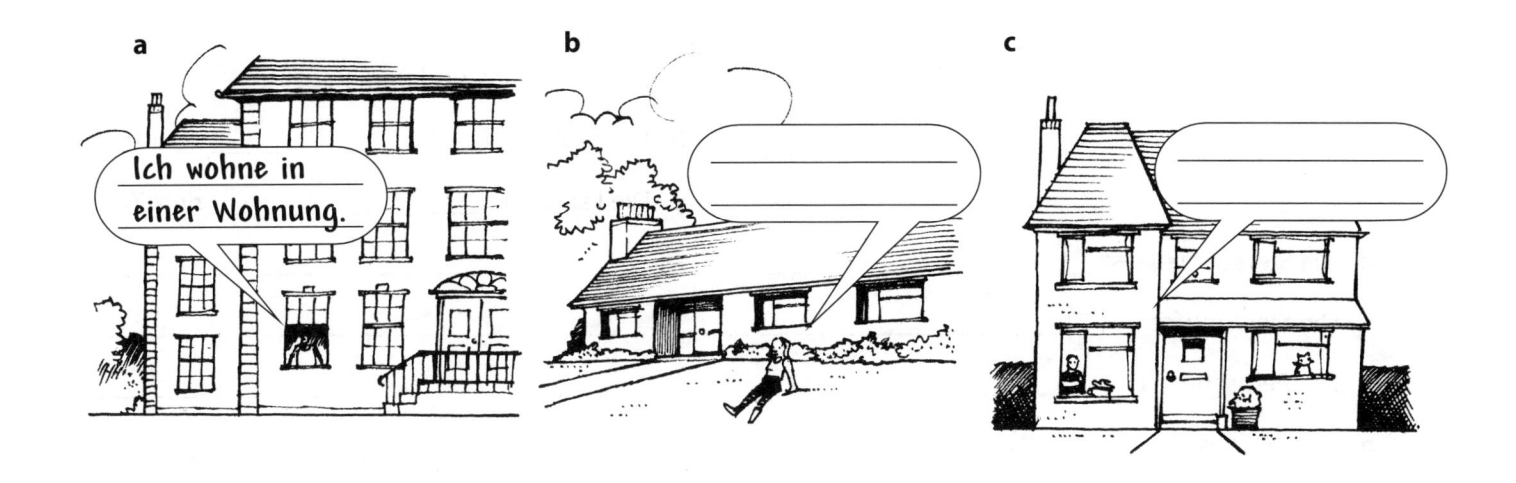

3 Was gibt es in deinem Zimmer?
What is there in your room?

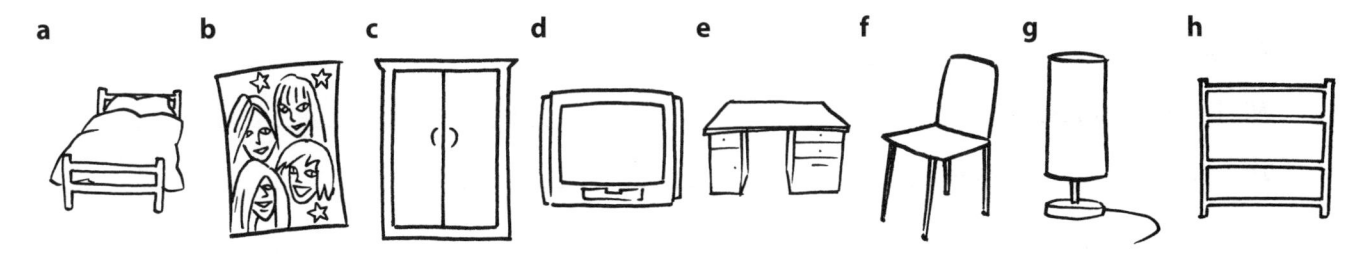

a b c d e f g h

Beispiel: *In meinem Zimmer gibt es …*

a ein Bett
b _____
c _____
d _____
e _____
f _____
g _____
h _____

fünfunddreißig **35**

Grammatik 2

Zu Hause

1 **Wo sind die Möbelstücke? Schreib die Sätze zu Ende.**
Complete these sentences to describe where the furniture is.

Flashback

auf **dem** Tisch **(masc.)**
neben **der** Lampe **(fem.)**
unter **dem** Bett **(neut.)**

Beispiel: Das Bett ist neben dem Kleiderschrank.

a Das Bett ist _____ dem Kleiderschrank und dem Regal.

b Der Stuhl ist _____ dem Tisch.

c Die Lampe ist _____ dem Tisch.

d Die Stereoanlage ist _____.

e Die Kleidung ist _____.

f Der Fernseher ist _____.

g Das Regal ist _____.

2 **Beantworte die Fragen auf Deutsch.**
Answer the questions in German for yourself.

Wo wohnst du? _____

Wie ist deine Adresse? _____

Was gibt es in deinem Haus? _____

_____

Wie ist dein Zimmer? _____

Was gibt es in deinem Zimmer? _____

_____

Wo sind die Möbelstücke? _____

_____

36 *sechsunddreißig*

Vokabular

Zu Hause

Meine Adresse — **My address**

Wo wohnst du? — Where do you live?
Wie ist deine Adresse? — What is your address?
Meine Adresse ist ... — My address is ...
Meine Hausnummer ist ... — My house number is ...
- zwanzig — twenty
- dreißig — thirty
- vierzig — forty
- fünfzig — fifty
- sechzig — sixty
- siebzig — seventy
- achtzig — eighty
- neunzig — ninety
- hundert — one hundred

Mein Haus — **My house**

Ich wohne ... — I live ...
- in einem Bungalow — in a bungalow
- in einem Einfamilienhaus — in a detached house
- in einem Doppelhaus — in a semi-detached house
- in einem Reihenhaus — in a terraced house
- in einer Wohnung — in a flat
- am Stadtrand — on the edge of town
- in einem Dorf — in a village
- in der Stadt — in the town
- in einer Wohnsiedlung — in a residential area
- auf dem Land — in the country

Und das ist die Küche ... — **And this is the kitchen ...**

das Badezimmer — the bathroom
die Dusche — the shower
das Esszimmer — the dining-room
die Garage — the garage
der Garten — the garden
der Keller — the cellar
die Küche — the kitchen
das Schlafzimmer — the bedroom

das Wohnzimmer — the living-room
im Erdgeschoss — on the ground floor
im ersten Stock — on the first floor
im zweiten Stock — on the second floor
In meinem Haus gibt es ein Esszimmer, einen Garten und eine Garage. — In my house there is a dining-room, a garden and a garage.

Mein Zimmer — **My room**

das Bett — the bed
der Computer — the computer
der Fernseher — the television
der Kleiderschrank — the wardrobe
die Lampe — the lamp
das Poster — the poster
das Regal — the shelf
der Schreibtisch — the desk
das Sofa — the sofa
die Stereoanlage — the stereo
der Stuhl — the chair
die Kleidung — the clothes
auf — on
hinter — behind
in — in
neben — next to
über — above
unter — under
vor — in front of
zwischen — between
In meinem Zimmer gibt es eine Stereoanlage. — In my room there is a stereo.
Die Stereoanlage ist auf dem Regal. — The stereo is on the shelf.
groß — big
modern — modern
klein — small
alt — old
unordentlich — untidy
schön — beautiful/pretty
hässlich — ugly

4 Kannst du …? Checklist

Zu Hause

This is a checklist of the things you should aim to learn in German using Klasse! neu 1. *Use the* **Check** *boxes and the* **Prove it!** *column to keep track of what you have learned.*

★ Tick the first box when you feel you are getting to grips with the learning objective, but sometimes need a prompt or time to think.

★ Tick the second box when you think you have fully mastered the learning objective and will be able to use it again in future.

★ Make notes following the prompts in the **Prove it!** column to help you show what you have learned. Your learning partner or parent can test you and initial the second box to confirm the progress you have made.

Learning objectives	Check		Prove it!
I can count up to 100.	☐	☐	*Get partner to test you.*
I can give my address and house number.	☐	☐	*Get partner to test you.*
I can ask someone for his/her address.	☐	☐	*Get partner to test you.*
I can describe where I live.	☐	☐	*Get partner to test you.*
I can ask someone about where he/she lives.	☐	☐	*Get partner to test you.*
I can describe my house or flat.	☐	☐	*Get partner to test you.*
I can say and write five different types of home.	☐	☐	*Write them down without looking at the book.*
I can say and write the names of different rooms in my home.	☐	☐	*Write them down without looking at the book.*
I can say where the different rooms are.	☐	☐	*Get partner to test you.*
I can say what is in my room.	☐	☐	*Get partner to test you.*
I can say where things are in my room.	☐	☐	*Get partner to test you.*
I can improve my reading skills by using a checklist.	☐	☐	*Explain to a partner.*
I can use a checklist to improve my written work.	☐	☐	*List three strategies that you would use here.*
I can work out some new words when reading.	☐	☐	*Explain to a partner three ways to do this.*
I know how to check my work for spellings and the gender of nouns.	☐	☐	*Explain to a partner three ways to do this.*
I can use the correct form of *ein/eine/ein* after *es gibt*.	☐	☐	*Explain the rule to a partner.*
I can use the correct form of *ein/eine/ein* after prepositions.	☐	☐	*Explain the rule to a partner.*

5.1 Etwas zum Essen

Guten Appetit!

1 Was ist alles in Cedis Kühlschrank?
Schreib die Wörter auf.

Write in the names of the items of food and drink in the fridge.

a _____   i _____

b _____   j _____

c _____   k _____

d _____   l _____

e _____   m _____

f _____   n _____

g _____   o _____

h _____

2 Was sagen sie? Füll die Lücken aus.

Fill in the gaps in the speech bubbles.

Sandra

Ich esse _____ mit _____ und _____ . Ich trinke _____ .

Ina

Ich esse _____ mit _____ und ich esse _____ und einen _____ . Ich trinke _____ .

Philipp

Ich esse _____ mit _____ und ich esse eine _____ . Ich trinke _____ .

neununddreißig **39**

5.2 Mahlzeit!

Guten Appetit!

1 Schreib die Wörter auf.
Write the correct items of food and drink.

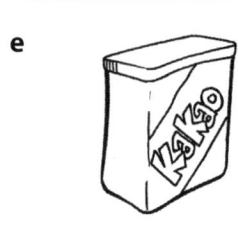

a, b, c, d, e, f, g, h, i, j, k, l, m, n, o, p

2 Mach eine Umfrage: „Was isst und trinkst du zum Frühstück, Mittagessen und Abendessen?" Schreib die Resultate auf.

Do a class survey: "What do you eat/drink for breakfast/lunch/dinner?" and write down the results.

Name	Frühstück	Mittagessen	Abendessen
Sarah	Müsli, Milch, Tee		

40 *vierzig*

5.3 Ich esse kein Fleisch!

Guten Appetit!

1 Was sagen sie? Schreib Sätze für die Bilder.
Write sentences for the pictures.

Beispiel:

a — Ich trinke gern Wasser.

b

c

d

e

2 Was isst und trinkt Tom nicht? Schreib Sprechblasen.
What does Tom not eat and drink? Write sentences for him.

a — Ich esse keinen Fisch!

b

c

d

e

f

einundvierzig **41**

5.4 Koch mit!

Guten Appetit!

1 Schau das Bild an und schreib Antworten für die Fragen.
Look at the picture and then answer the questions.

a Was macht Jan?
_____
_____
_____.

b Was isst Mia nicht?
_____
_____
_____.

c Was ist Tims Lieblingsessen?
_____
_____
_____
_____.

2 Lies Ullis E-Mail und finde die passenden Bilder.
Read Ulli's e-mail and match the pictures to the people.

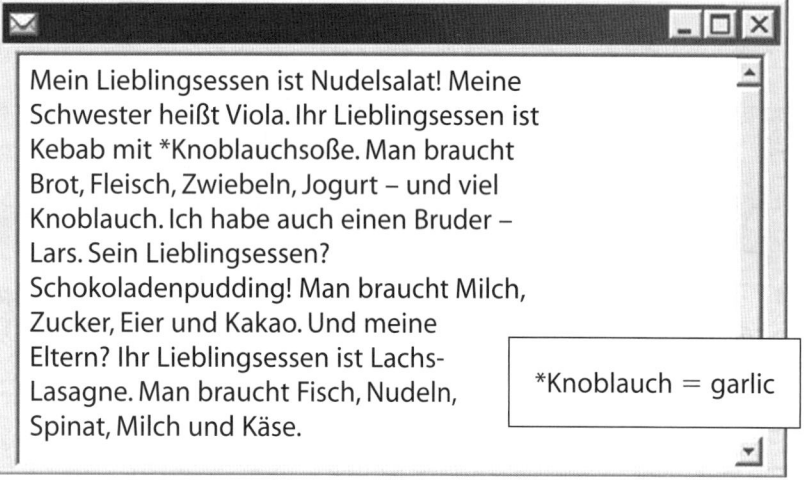

> Mein Lieblingsessen ist Nudelsalat! Meine Schwester heißt Viola. Ihr Lieblingsessen ist Kebab mit *Knoblauchsoße. Man braucht Brot, Fleisch, Zwiebeln, Jogurt – und viel Knoblauch. Ich habe auch einen Bruder – Lars. Sein Lieblingsessen? Schokoladenpudding! Man braucht Milch, Zucker, Eier und Kakao. Und meine Eltern? Ihr Lieblingsessen ist Lachs-Lasagne. Man braucht Fisch, Nudeln, Spinat, Milch und Käse.

*Knoblauch = garlic

Eltern ☐   Lars ☐   Viola ☐

3 Was ist <u>dein</u> Lieblingsessen? Was braucht man? Schreib eine Einkaufsliste.
Write a shopping list for <u>your</u> favourite meal.

_____
_____
_____
_____

42 zweiundvierzig

Grammatik 1

Guten Appetit!

1 Schreib Sätze für die Bilder.
Write sentences for the pictures.

Flashback

Ich esse Obst.
→ Ich esse **gern** Obst.
→ Ich esse **nicht gern** Obst.

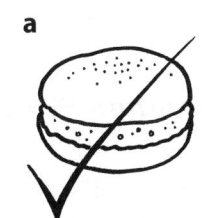

Beispiel:

a Ich esse gern Hamburger.
b _____
c _____
d _____
e _____
f _____

2 Schreib die passenden Wörter auf.
Write the correct words (keinen/keine/kein).

a Ich trinke _____ Orangensaft.
b Ich esse _____ Wurst.
c Ich trinke _____ Tee.
d Ich esse _____ Cornflakes.
e Ich esse _____ Gemüse.
f Ich trinke _____ Milch.

Flashback

masculine	→	Ich esse **keinen** Käse.
feminine	→	Ich trinke **keine** Milch.
neuter	→	Ich esse **kein** Brot.
plural	→	Ich esse **keine** Pommes frites.

3 Was isst/trinkst du nicht? Schreib Sätze für die neuen Wörter.
Write sentences with keinen/keine/kein *for the new words.*

a die Limonade
b der Blumenkohl
c die Pralinen (pl.)
d der Kakao
e das Schnitzel
f die Kirschen

Beispiel:

a Ich trinke keine Limonade.
b _____
c _____
d _____
e _____
f _____

dreiundvierzig **43**

Grammatik 2

Guten Appetit!

Flashback

	my	*your*	*his*	*her*	
masculine	mein	dein	sein	ihr	Jogurt
feminine	meine	deine	seine	ihre	Wurst
neuter	mein	dein	sein	ihr	Eis

1a Unterstreiche alle Maskulin-Wörter in Blau, alle Feminin-Wörter in Rot und alle Neutrum-Wörter in Grün.

Underline all masculine words in blue, all feminine words in red and all neuter words in green.

1 Salat   2 Pizza   3 Lehrer   4 Cola   5 Lieblingsessen   6 Fleisch

1b Schreib die Wörter in Übung 1a mit *mein(e)/dein(e)/sein(e)/ihr(e)* auf.

Write the words in activity 1a with mein(e)/dein(e)/sein(e)/ihr(e).

1 _____ (my)   4 _____ (your)

2 _____ (her)   5 _____ (my)

3 _____ (his)   6 _____ (her)

2 Füll die Lücken aus.

Fill in the gaps with the correct pronouns.

a _____ Bruder isst gern Zwiebeln, Jasmin?

b Kathi isst gern – _____ Lieblingsessen ist Pizza.

c Das sind meine Brüder – _____ Lieblingsessen ist Pizza mit Thunfisch.

d Und Andi? Hier – das ist _____ Lieblingssalat!

e _____ Mutter isst am liebsten Gulasch.

f Hier ist _____ Wurst, Cedi!

Vokabular

Guten Appetit!

Ich esse/trinke …	***I'm eating/drinking …***	Zum Mittagessen trinke ich Wasser.	*For lunch I drink water.*
Was isst du?	*What are you eating?*	Zum Abendessen trinke ich Tee.	*For dinner I drink tea.*
Was trinkst du?	*What are you drinking?*		
Ich esse …	*I'm eating …*	**Was isst/trinkst du gern?**	***What do you like to eat/drink?***
einen Apfel	*an apple*		
eine Banane	*a banana*	Was isst du gern?	*What do you like to eat?*
Brot/Brötchen	*bread/bread rolls*	Was trinkst du gern?	*What do you like to drink?*
Fisch	*fish*	Was isst du nicht gern?	*What don't you like to eat?*
ein Ei	*an egg*	Was trinkst du nicht gern?	*What don't you like to drink?*
Jogurt	*yoghurt*	Ich esse (nicht) gern …	*I (don't) like to eat …*
Käse	*cheese*	Fleisch	*meat*
Kartoffeln	*potatoes*	Gemüse	*vegetables*
Nudeln	*pasta*	Obst	*fruit*
Salat	*salad*	Pommes frites	*fries/chips*
Wurst	*sausage*	Ich trinke (nicht) gern …	*I (don't) like to drink …*
Ich trinke …	*I'm drinking …*	Kaffee	*coffee*
Cola	*coke*	Milch	*milk*
Milch	*milk*	Ich esse …	*I …*
Orangensaft	*orange juice*	keinen Fisch	*don't eat fish*
Mahlzeiten	***Meals***	keine Wurst	*don't eat sausage*
Wass isst du …	*What do you eat …*	kein Gemüse	*don't eat vegetables*
zum Frühstück?	*for breakfast?*	keine Pommes frites	*don't eat fries/chips*
zum Mittagessen?	*for lunch?*	Ich trinke …	*I …*
zum Abendessen?	*for dinner?*	keinen Kaffee	*don't drink coffee*
Ich esse normalerweise Brot.	*I usually eat bread.*	keine Milch	*don't drink milk*
Ich esse meistens Nudeln.	*I mainly eat pasta.*	kein Wasser	*don't drink water*
Zum Frühstück esse ich …	*For breakfast I eat …*	**Kochen**	***Cooking***
Cornflakes/Müsli	*cornflakes/muesli*	Ich mache Pizza mit …	*I'm making a pizza with …*
Brot mit Marmelade	*bread with jam*	Ei	*egg*
Brötchen mit Honig	*bread rolls with honey*	Paprika	*peppers*
Zum Mittagessen esse ich …	*For lunch I eat …*	Pilzen	*mushrooms*
Hähnchen mit Reis	*chicken with rice*	Schinken	*ham*
Zum Abendessen esse ich …	*For dinner I eat …*	Thunfisch	*tuna*
Brot mit Butter und Käse	*bread with butter and cheese*	Wurst	*sausage*
Was trinkst du …	*What do you drink …*	Man braucht …	*You need …*
zum Frühstück/ Mittagessen/ Abendessen?	*for breakfast/ lunch/dinner?*	Käse	*cheese*
		Pilze	*mushrooms*
		Spinat	*spinach*
		Tomaten	*tomatoes*
Zum Frühstück trinke ich Kaffee.	*For breakfast I drink coffee.*	Zwiebeln	*onions*
		Mein Lieblingsessen ist …	*My favourite food is …*
		Pizza mit Thunfisch	*pizza with tuna*

fünfundvierzig **45**

5 Kannst du …? Checklist

Guten Appetit!

This is a checklist of the things you should aim to learn in German using Klasse! neu 1. Use the **Check** boxes and the **Prove it!** column to keep track of what you have learned.

★ Tick the first box when you feel you are getting to grips with the learning objective, but sometimes need a prompt or time to think.

★ Tick the second box when you think you have fully mastered the learning objective and will be able to use it again in future.

★ Make notes following the prompts in the **Prove it!** column to help you show what you have learned. Your learning partner or parent can test you and initial the second box to confirm the progress you have made.

Learning objectives	Check	Prove it!
I can say what I eat and drink.	☐ ☐	*Get partner to test you.*
I can say what I don't eat and drink.	☐ ☐	*Get partner to test you.*
I can say what I eat and drink for different meals.	☐ ☐	*Get partner to test you.*
I can ask someone what he/she eats and drinks for different meals.	☐ ☐	*Get partner to test you.*
I can say when I eat and drink different meals.	☐ ☐	*Get partner to test you.*
I can ask someone when he/she eats and drinks different meals.	☐ ☐	*Get partner to test you.*
I can say what I like and don't like to eat and drink.	☐ ☐	*Get partner to test you.*
I can ask someone what he/she likes to eat and drink.	☐ ☐	*Get partner to test you.*
I can talk about my favourite food.	☐ ☐	*Get partner to test you.*
I can talk about my favourite recipes.	☐ ☐	*Get partner to test you.*
I can use the German–English section of a dictionary.	☐ ☐	*Find the English for these words:* Mittagessen, Kartoffeln, Wurst.
I can use the English–German section of a dictionary.	☐ ☐	*Find the German for these words:* pear, cake, onions.
I can use *mein, dein, sein, ihr* with the right endings.	☐ ☐	*How do you say:* 'That's my milk!' 'What's her favourite ice cream?' 'Is that your salad?' *in German?*
I can recognize the difference in sounds between a long and a short *o* and a long and a short *u*.	☐ ☐	*Say these words aloud:* Limonade, Honig, Hunger, Nudeln.

6.1 Was spielst du gern?

Meine Interessen

1 Was spielst du? Füll die Lücken aus.
Fill in the gaps in the speech bubbles.

Ich spiele …

a, b, c, d, e, f, g, h, i

2 Lies Evas E-Mail und lies die Sätze. Sind sie richtig (R), falsch (F) oder nicht im Text (N)?
Read Eva's e-mail. Are the sentences true, false or not in the text?

> Ich bin sehr musikalisch – ich spiele Saxofon und ich spiele auch gern Gitarre.
> Mein Bruder Johann spielt nicht gern Gitarre, aber er spielt gern Schlagzeug. Er spielt auch gern Rugby und er spielt gern Fußball.
> Ich bin auch sportlich – ich spiele gern Basketball und ich spiele Volleyball, aber ich spiele nicht gern Tennis.

R F N

a Eva ist nicht musikalisch.
b Ihr Bruder spielt Saxofon.
c Johann ist sportlich.
d Eva spielt gern Rugby.
e Sie spielt Volleyball und Basketball.
f Sie spielt nicht gern Tennis.

siebenundvierzig **47**

6.2 Hobbys

Meine Interessen

1 Was machen sie gern/nicht gern? Schreib Sätze für die Bilder.
What do they like/not like doing? Write sentences for the pictures.

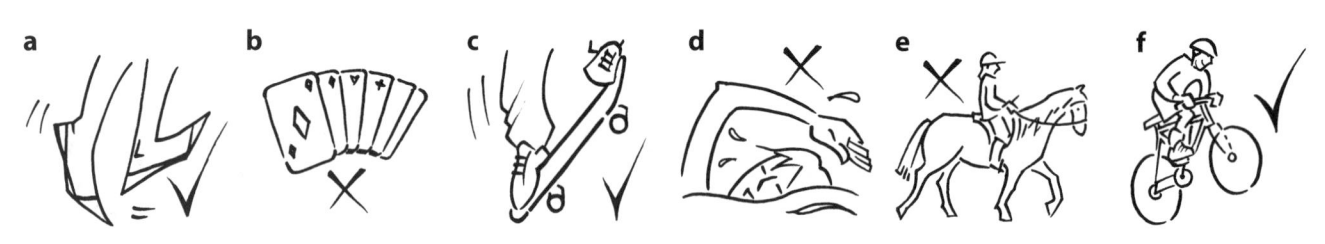

a   Ich tanze gern.
b   Ihr
c   Er
d   Wir
e   Sie (pl.)
f   Du

2 Was machst du gern/nicht gern? Schreib Sätze für die Bilder.
What do you like/not like doing? Write sentences for the pictures.

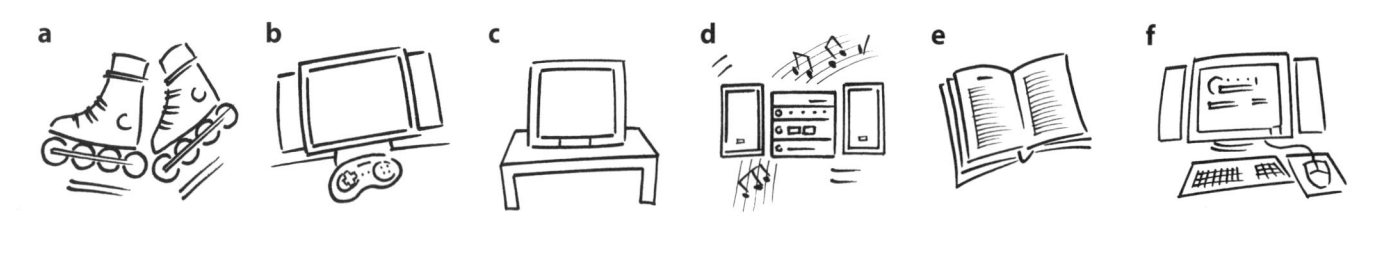

a
b
c
d
e
f

3 Du bist dran – schreib Sätze.
Write sentences to say which other things you like doing.

48 achtundvierzig

6.3 Ich sehe gern fern!

Meine Interessen

1 Was für eine Sendung ist das? Schreib die passenden Wörter mit *ein/eine/ein* auf.
Write the correct words with ein/eine/ein.

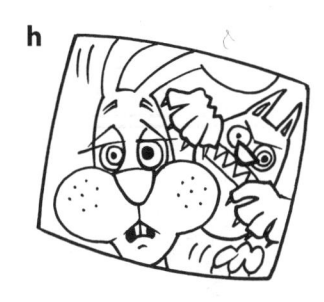

a _____ b _____ c _____ d _____

e _____ f _____ g _____ h _____

2 Lies Hannahs E-Mail und die Steckbriefe A und B. Ist Hannah A oder B?
Read Hannah's e-mail and the two cards. Is Hannah A or B?

> Ich heiße Hannah und ich bin 14 Jahre alt. Mein Lieblingshobby? Ich sehe gern fern! Ich sehe am liebsten Seifenopern – sie sind super! Ich höre auch gern Musik und ich sehe gern Musiksendungen. Und ich sehe gern Dokumentarfilme – sie sind interessant. Ich finde auch Talkshows spannend. Aber ich finde Sportsendungen doof – ich bin nicht sportlich.

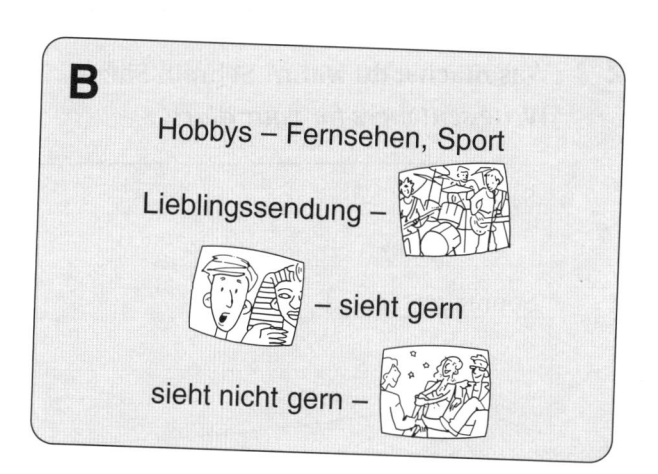

A
Hobbys – Fernsehen, Musik
Lieblingssendung –
– sieht gern:
sieht nicht gern –

B
Hobbys – Fernsehen, Sport
Lieblingssendung –
– sieht gern
sieht nicht gern –

6.4 Wie oft machst du …?

Meine Interessen

1 Was macht Maxi-Monster wann? Schreib Sprechblasen.
What does Maxi-Monster do when? Write sentences.

7.00 — Um 7 Uhr schwimme ich.

13.00

16.00

18.00

19.00

20.00

2 Was machst du wann? Schreib Sätze.
Write sentences for your diary.

Samstag:	Montag–Freitag
	morgens: Ich höre Musik.
Sonntag:	nachmittags:
	abends:
	vor der Schule:
	nach der Schule:

50 fünfzig

Grammatik 1

Meine Interessen

Flashback

The present tense endings of regular verbs follow this pattern:

schreiben

ich schreib**e**	wir schreib**en**
du schreib**st**	ihr schreib**t**
er/sie/es schreib**t**	sie/Sie schreib**en**

1 Füll die Lücken für *finden* aus.
Fill in the correct verb endings for the regular verb finden.

Ich _____ Sport super, aber du _____ Tennis langweilig! Sarah _____ Golf interessant – und wir _____ Rugby toll! Und wie _____ ihr Basketball? Tom und Mia _____ Fußball doof!

2 Füll die Lücken aus.
Fill in the verb forms.

a Wir _____ eine E-Mail.

b Er _____ Kai.

c Sie _____ Tennis.

d Ich _____ Pizza.

e _____ ihr ein Eis?

f Wo _____ du?

einundfünfzig **51**

Grammatik 2

6   *Meine Interessen*

> **Flashback**
>
> Some irregular verbs also change their spellings in the *du* and *er/sie/es* forms:
>
> | | **lesen** | **sehen** | **fahren** |
> |---|---|---|---|
> | ich | lese | sehe | fahre |
> | du | liest | siehst | fährst |
> | er/sie/es | liest | sieht | fährt |
> | | e → ie | | a → ä |

1   Finde sechs Sätze.
Draw lines to join the beginnings and ends of sentences.

a	Ich	1	fährt nicht gern Rad.
b	Du	2	lese eine E-Mail.
c	Er	3	seht abends fern.
d	Wir	4	liest gern.
e	Ihr	5	fahren Skateboard.
f	Sie	6	sehen nicht gern fern.

2   Finde die passenden Bilder und füll die Lücken aus.
Draw lines to the correct pictures and fill in the gaps.

1   a   Du f_____ gern Rollschuh.

2   b   Ich l_____ nicht gern.

3   c   Wir s_____ gern fern.

4   d   Er f_____ morgens Rad.

5   e   Du l_____ einen Brief.

6   f   Sie s_____ gern Seifenopern.

Vokabular

Meine Interessen

Was spielst du gern? / What do you like playing?

Was spielst du gern? — What do you like playing?

Ich spiele gern … — I like playing …
- Basketball/Fußball/Golf/ — basketball/football/golf/
- Tennis/Volleyball/Rugby/ — tennis/volleyball/rugby/
- Klavier/Geige/Gitarre/ — piano/violin/guitar/
- Trompete/Saxofon/Schlagzeug — trumpet/saxophone/drums

Hobbys / Hobbies

Was ist dein Hobby? — What's your hobby?
Was sind deine Hobbys? — What are your hobbies?
Ich lese./Ich reite./Ich schwimme. — I read./I ride./I swim.
Ich tanze. — I dance.
Ich spiele … — I play …
- Computerspiele — computer games
- Karten — cards

Ich fahre Skateboard/Rad/Rollschuh. — I go skateboarding/cycling/rollerskating.
Ich höre Musik. — I listen to music.
Ich surfe im Internet. — I surf the Internet.

Fernsehen / TV

Was für eine Sendung ist das? — What kind of programme is that?
Das ist … — That is …
- ein Film — a film
- ein Dokumentarfilm — a documentary
- ein Trickfilm — a cartoon film
- eine Musiksendung — a music programme
- eine Talkshow — a talk show
- eine Seifenoper — a soap opera
- eine Serie — a series
- eine Sportsendung — a sports programme

Das sind die Nachrichten. — That's the news.
Wie findest du Filme? — What do you think of films?
Siehst du gern Serien? — Do you like watching series?
Was ist deine Lieblingssendung? — What's your favourite programme?
Ich finde … — I find …
Das ist … — That's …
- lustig/spannend — funny/exciting
- interessant — interesting
- blöd/doof — stupid
- langweilig — boring

Ich sehe (nicht) gern … — I (don't) like watching …
Meine Lieblingssendung ist … — My favourite programme is …

Wie oft/wann? / How often/when?

Wie spät ist es? — What time is it?
Was machst du um … Uhr? — What are you doing at … o'clock?
Wie oft machst du Sport? — How often do you do sport?
Wie oft spielst du Karten? — How often do you play cards?
Wie oft siehst du fern? — How often do you watch TV?

jeden Tag — every day
jeden Morgen — every morning
jeden Nachmittag — every afternoon
jeden Abend — every evening
morgens — in the morning
nachmittags — in the afternoon
abends — in the evening
am Wochenende — at the weekend
am Montag — on Monday
einmal pro Woche — once a week
zweimal pro Monat — twice a month

dreiundfünfzig 53

6 Kannst du …? Checklist

Meine Interessen

This is a checklist of the things you should aim to learn in German using Klasse! neu 1. *Use the* **Check** *boxes and the* **Prove it!** *column to keep track of what you have learned.*

★ Tick the first box when you feel you are getting to grips with the learning objective, but sometimes need a prompt or time to think.

★ Tick the second box when you think you have fully mastered the learning objective and will be able to use it again in future.

★ Make notes following the prompts in the **Prove it!** column to help you show what you have learned. Your learning partner or parent can test you and initial the second box to confirm the progress you have made.

Learning objectives	Check		Prove it!
I can say which sports and musical instruments I play.	☐	☐	*Get partner to test you.*
I can talk about my hobbies.	☐	☐	*Get partner to test you.*
I can ask someone about his/her hobbies.	☐	☐	*Get partner to test you.*
I can say what I like/don't like doing.	☐	☐	*Get partner to test you.*
I can ask someone what he/she likes/doesn't like doing.	☐	☐	*Get partner to test you.*
I can ask about TV programmes.	☐	☐	*Get partner to test you.*
I can describe TV programmes.	☐	☐	*Get partner to test you.*
I can ask for and give opinions about TV programmes.	☐	☐	*Get partner to test you.*
I can say when and how often I do something.	☐	☐	*Get partner to test you.*
I can ask someone about when and how often he/she does something.	☐	☐	*Get partner to test you.*
I can form the present tense of regular verbs.	☐	☐	*Ask your partner three questions about hobbies.*
I can use the correct word order with time expressions at the beginning of a sentence.	☐	☐	*Explain to a partner.*
I can recognize the different sounds *sp* and *sch*.	☐	☐	*Say these words aloud:* Sport, Schule, spricht, schreibt.

7.1 Woher kommst du?

Meine Stadt

Beispiel:

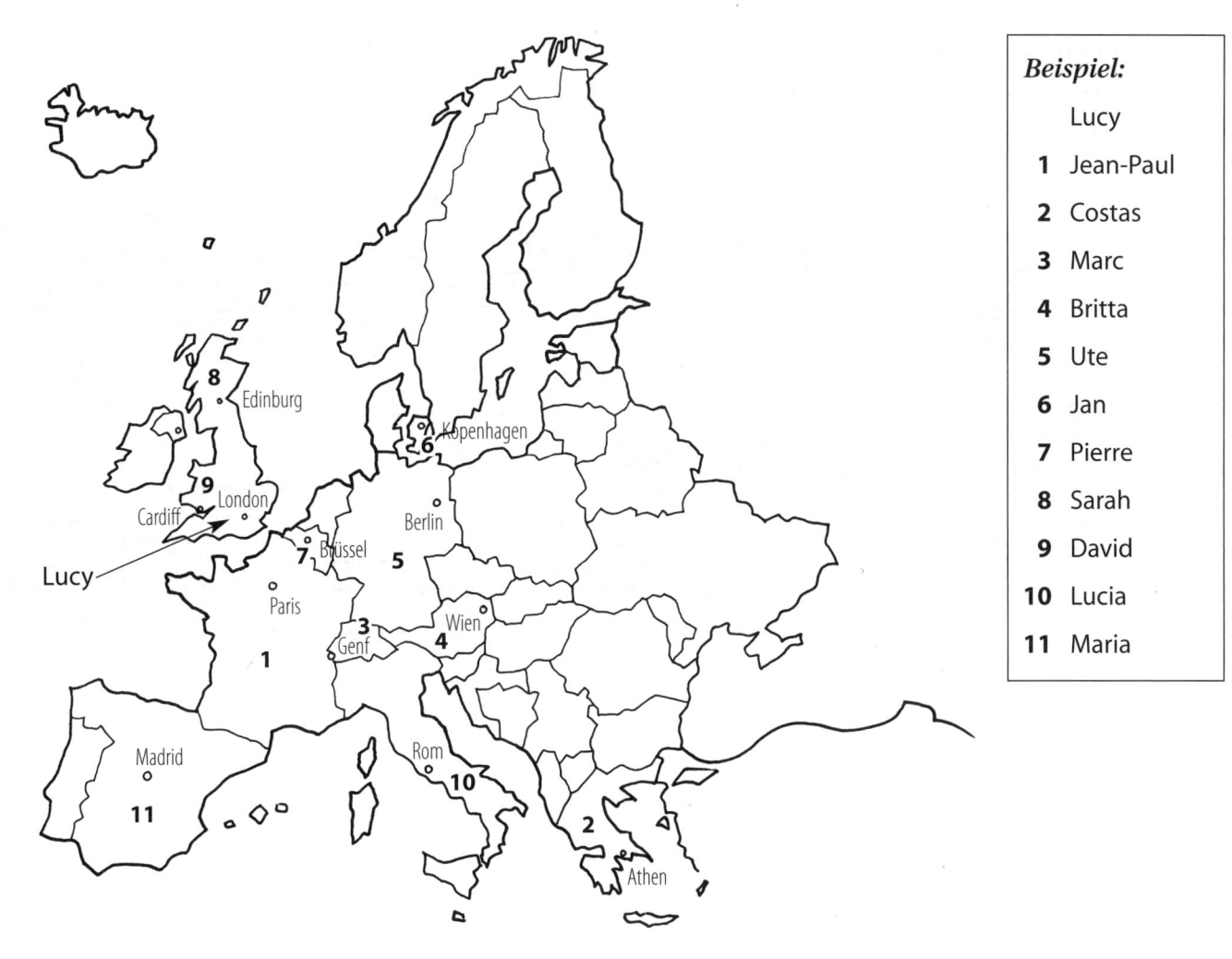

	Lucy
1	Jean-Paul
2	Costas
3	Marc
4	Britta
5	Ute
6	Jan
7	Pierre
8	Sarah
9	David
10	Lucia
11	Maria

1 Wo wohnen diese Jugendlichen? Schreib Sätze.
Where do these teenagers live? Write sentences.

Beispiel: Lucy: Ich komme aus England. Ich wohne in London. Das ist im Süden.

1 _____
2 _____
3 _____
4 _____
5 _____
6 _____
7 _____
8 _____
9 _____
10 _____
11 _____

fünfundfünfzig **55**

7.2 Was gibt es in Hollfeld?
Meine Stadt

1 Was gibt es in dieser Stadt?
Describe what there is in this town.

Es gibt … ein modernes Sportzentrum, _____

_____

2a Lies Tanjas E-Mail. Richtig oder falsch?
Read Tanja's e-mail. True or false?

> Hallo! Ich bin Tanja und ich wohne in Mössingen in Deutschland. Mössingen ist eine kleine Stadt im Südwesten in der Nähe von Stuttgart. In Mössingen gibt es ein modernes Schwimmbad und ein kleines Kino. Es gibt auch einen tollen Markt am Samstag und einen schönen Park. Wir haben auch eine alte Kirche und ein neues Rathaus, aber kein Museum und keine Disco – schade!

		R	F
a	Mössingen ist eine kleine Stadt.	☐	☐
b	Mössingen liegt im Norden.	☐	☐
c	Das Schwimmbad ist modern.	☐	☐
d	Es gibt kein Kino.	☐	☐
e	Der Markt ist sehr gut.	☐	☐
f	Die Kirche ist alt.	☐	☐
g	Es gibt ein interessantes Museum.	☐	☐

2b Korrigiere die falschen Sätze.
Correct the false sentences.

_____

_____

56 *sechsundfünfzig*

7.3 Was kann man hier machen? — *Meine Stadt*

1 Schreib Sätze für die Bilder. Man kann…
Describe the pictures.

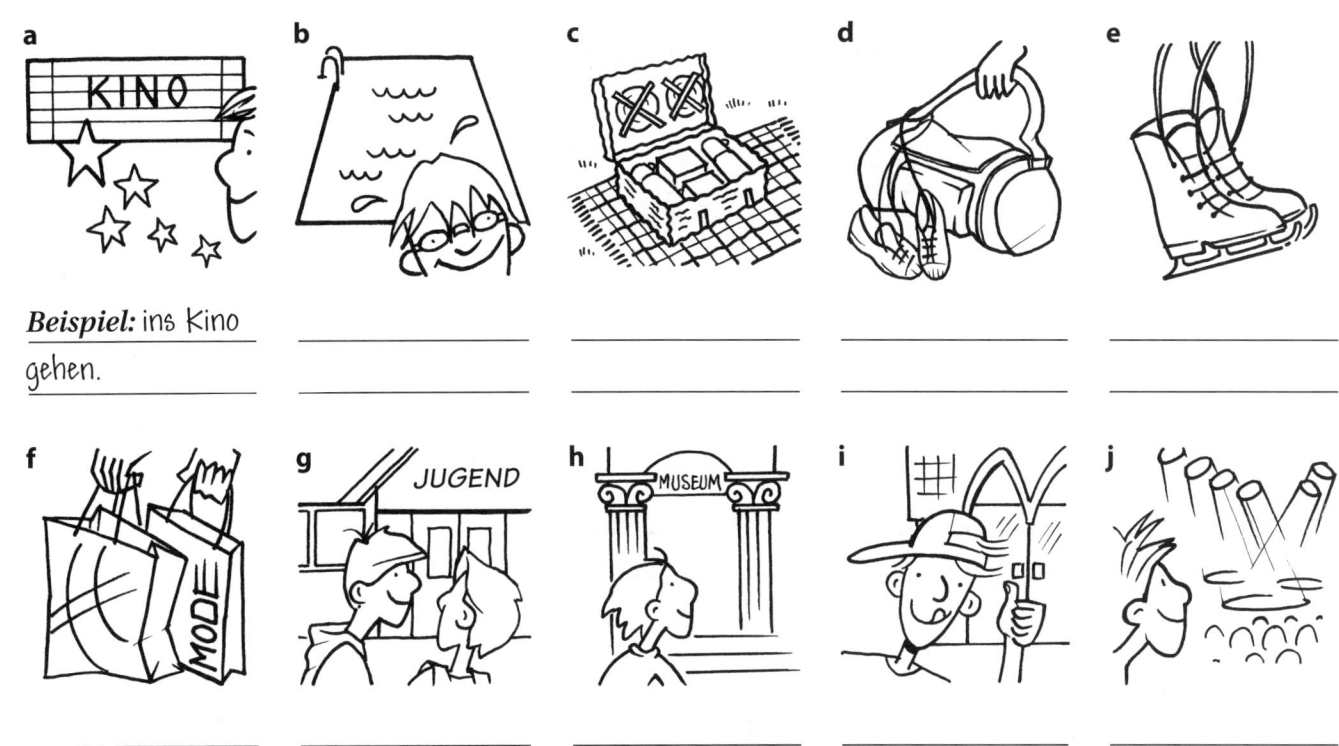

Beispiel: ins Kino gehen.

2 Lies Tanjas E-Mail. Ist das Mössingen oder Stuttgart?
Read Tanja's e-mail. Is she talking about Mössingen or Stuttgart? Write M or S below each picture.

In Mössingen kann man nicht sehr viel machen – man kann ins Kino oder ins Schwimmbad gehen oder zum Jugendzentrum gehen. Aber in Stuttgart gibt es viel zu tun. Man kann auf die Eisbahn gehen oder ins Popkonzert gehen. Es gibt viele Geschäfte und man kann einen tollen Einkaufsbummel machen. Es gibt auch ein interessantes Museum oder man kann das Schloss besuchen. Das Schloss hat einen schönen Park und man kann dort ein Picknick machen. Aber man kann auch ins Fastfood-Restaurant gehen – in Mössingen kann man das nicht machen.

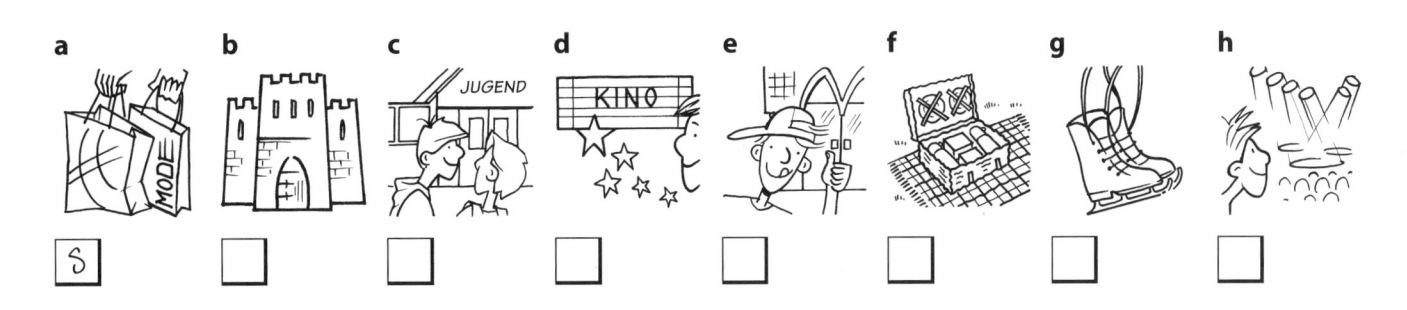

a: S

siebenundfünfzig 57

7.4 Wie fährst du in die Stadt?

Meine Stadt

1 Schreib die Sätze richtig auf.
Write the sentences in the correct order.

1 Auto | fahre | mit | Ich | dem | .   Ich fahre mit dem Auto.
2 mit | Fährst | der | du | U-Bahn | ? _____
3 dem | Wir | Zug | mit | fahren | .   _____
4 Fuß | gehe | zu | Ich | .   _____
5 der | mit | du | Straßenbahn | Fährst | ?   _____
6 Wir | Rad | dem | fahren | mit | .   _____
7 mit | Bus | Ich | dem | fahre | .   _____

2 Finde jetzt die passenden Bilder für die Sätze in Übung 1.
Find the matching pictures for the sentences in activity 1.

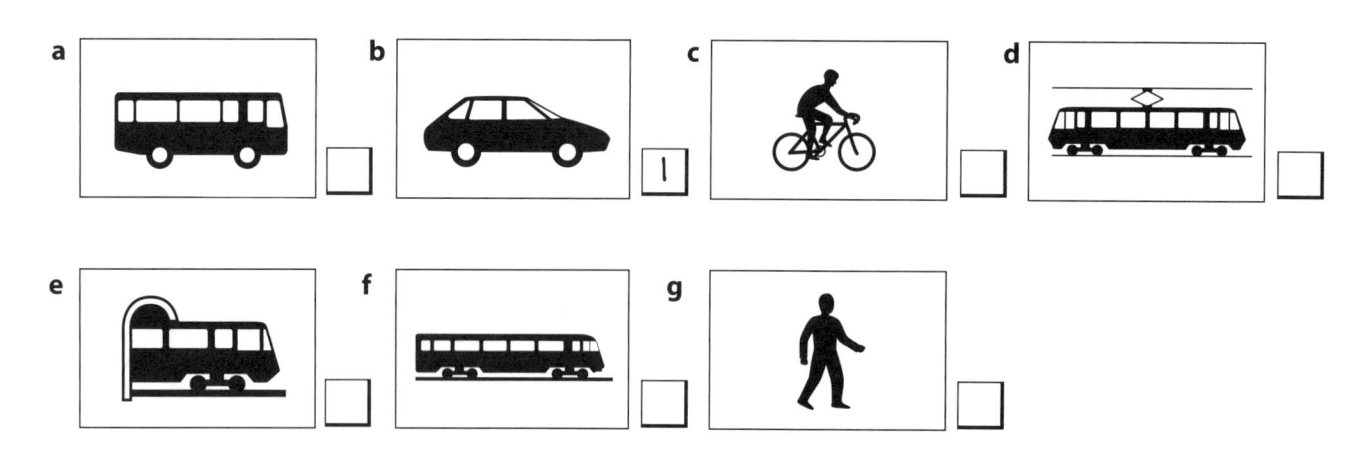

a b c (1) d e f g

3 Lies Angelikas Text und beantworte die Fragen.
Read Angelika's text and answer the questions.

> Es ist Samstag und ich fahre mit dem Bus in die Stadt – eine Fahrkarte hin und zurück kostet zwei Euro zwanzig. Das ist NICHT billig! In der Stadt kaufe ich CDs. Ich gehe nachmittags zu Fuß mit Katja zum Sportzentrum. Und abends? Wir gehen in die Disco oder ins Kino.

a Wie fährt Angelika in die Stadt? _____
b Was kostet eine Fahrkarte? _____
c Was kauft sie in der Stadt? _____
d Wohin geht sie nachmittags? _____
e Was macht sie abends? _____

58 achtundfünfzig

Grammatik 1

Meine Stadt

Flashback

m. **Der** Bahnhof ist groß. → Bayreuth hat **einen großen** Bahnhof.
f. **Die** Kirche ist klein. → Es gibt **eine kleine** Kirche.
n. **Das** Sportzentrum ist modern. → Es gibt **ein modernes** Sportzentrum.

1 Füll die Lücken aus.
Fill in the gaps.

In meiner Stadt gibt es ein_____ toll_____ Markt, ein_____ groß_____ Bank, ein_____ schön_____ Dom, ein_____ modern_____ Theater, ein_____ alt_____ Bahnhof, ein_____ toll_____ Sportzentrum und ein_____ alt_____ Rathaus.

2 Was gibt es in dieser Stadt?
Describe what there is in this town.

Beispiel:

a — neu
b — modern
c — alt
d — schön
e — groß
f — klein

Es gibt eine neue Disco.

7 Grammatik 2

Meine Stadt

Flashback

der Park → Ich fahre mit dem Bus **zum** Park.
die Schule → Ich fahre mit der Straßenbahn **zur** Schule.
das Schwimmbad → Ich fahre mit dem Rad **zum** Schwimmbad.

1 *zum* oder *zur*? Schreib die Wörter auf.
zum or zur? Write the words in the box in the correct place.

Schule   Kirche   Rathaus
Sportzentrum   Disco   Kino
Bank   Schloss   Park   Markt
Hallenbad   Dom   Bahnhof

ZUM

Schule

ZUR

2 Lies die Sätze. Wer sind 1–6?
Read the sentences to work out who 1–6 are in the grid.

Dieter geht nicht zum Markt.
Sven hat kein Auto.
Frau Haab fährt gern mit dem Auto.
Sven geht zu Fuß zum Markt.

Herr Albrecht hat kein Rad.
Mustafa fährt gern mit dem Rad.
Sabina fährt mit dem Auto zum Kino.
Mustafa fährt mit der Straßenbahn zum Kino.

60 sechzig

Vokabular

Meine Stadt

Woher kommst du?	**Where do you come from?**	das Theater	the theatre
		modern	modern
Ich komme aus ...	I come from ...	neu	new
England	England	alt	old
Schottland	Scotland	interessant	interesting
Irland	Ireland	groß	big
Wales	Wales	toll	great, super
Deutschland	Germany	schön	beautiful
Österreich	Austria	klein	small
der Schweiz	Switzerland		
Frankreich	France	**Was kann man in Bayreuth machen?**	**What can you do in Bayreuth?**
Belgien	Belgium		
Holland	Holland	Man kann ...	You can ...
Spanien	Spain	ins Museum gehen	go to the museum
Italien	Italy	ins Jugendzentrum gehen	go to the youth centre
Portugal	Portugal	einen Einkaufsbummel machen	go shopping
Griechenland	Greece	ins Sportzentrum gehen	go to the sports centre
Dänemark	Denmark	ins Fast-food Restaurant gehen.	go to a fast food restaurant.
im Norden	in the north	ins Popkonzert gehen	go to a pop concert
im Süden	in the south	ins Schwimmbad gehen	go to the (outdoor) swimming-pool
im Westen	in the west	ins Hallenbad gehen	go to the (indoor) swimming-pool
im Osten	in the east	auf die Eisbahn gehen	go to the ice rink
im Nordosten	in the north-east	ins Kino gehen	go to the cinema
im Nordwesten	in the north-west	ein Picknick machen	have a picnic
im Südosten	in the south-east	das Schloss besuchen	visit the castle
im Südwesten	in the south-west		
		Wie fährst du in die Stadt?	**How do you travel to town?**
Willkommen in Hollfeld	**Welcome to Hollfeld**		
		Ich fahre ...	I travel ...
der Bahnhof	the station	mit dem Bus	by bus
der Dom	the cathedral	mit dem Auto	by car
der Markt	the market	mit dem Zug	by train
der Park	the park	mit dem Rad	by bike
die Bank	the bank	mit der U-Bahn	by underground
die Disco	the disco	mit der Straßenbahn	by tram
die Kirche	the church	Ich gehe zu Fuß	I walk
die Post	the post office		
das Hallenbad	the (indoor) swimming-pool		
das Schwimmbad	the (outdoor) swimming-pool		
das Kino	the cinema		
das Rathaus	the town hall		
das Schloss	the castle		
das Sportzentrum	the sports centre		

7 Kannst du ...? Checklist

Meine Stadt

This is a checklist of the things you should aim to learn in German using Klasse! neu 1. Use the **Check** boxes and the **Prove it!** column to keep track of what you have learned.

★ Tick the first box when you feel you are getting to grips with the learning objective, but sometimes need a prompt or time to think.

★ Tick the second box when you think you have fully mastered the learning objective and will be able to use it again in future.

★ Make notes following the prompts in the **Prove it!** column to help you show what you have learned. Your learning partner or parent can test you and initial the second box to confirm the progress you have made.

Learning objectives	Check	Prove it!
I can say the names of different European countries.	☐ ☐	*Get partner to test you.*
I can say which country I come from.	☐ ☐	*Get partner to test you.*
I can describe where my town is.	☐ ☐	*Get partner to test you.*
I can ask where somebody comes from.	☐ ☐	*Get partner to test you.*
I can describe the public buildings in my town or village.	☐ ☐	*Get partner to test you.*
I can describe what the town and buildings are like.	☐ ☐	*Get partner to test you.*
I can use the correct endings for adjectives after *Es gibt ...*	☐ ☐	*Without looking at the book, write down 'There is a beautiful cathedral, a modern sports centre and an old church'.*
I can say what activities you can do in a town.	☐ ☐	*Get partner to test you.*
I can ask which means of transport someone uses.	☐ ☐	*Get partner to test you.*
I can say which means of transport I use.	☐ ☐	*Get partner to test you.*
I can say where I am going.	☐ ☐	*Get partner to test you.*
I can recognize the different sounds *s, ß, sch, st*.	☐ ☐	*Say these words aloud:* Schule, super, Stadt, Fuß.
I can recognize the different sounds *ü, ö*.	☐ ☐	*Say these words aloud:* Göttingen, Übung, öffnen, Überlingen.

62 zweiundsechzig

8.1 Wie ist das Wetter?

Meine Freizeit

1a Lies den Wetterbericht. Welche Karte ist das? A oder B?
Read the weather report. Which map is it describing?

> Heute ist es sonnig in Leipzig, aber nicht in Berlin: es ist windig. In München ist es frostig. In Stuttgart ist es auch frostig und es schneit. Es regnet in Köln und in Hamburg ist es auch nicht schön. In Hamburg ist es bewölkt.

1b Schreib den Wetterbericht für die andere Karte.
Write the weather report for the other map.

Heute schneit es in München, ...

2a Welche drei Bilder sind das?
Which three pictures are being described?

a   b   c   d   e   f

1 Wenn es heiß ist, fahre ich Rad.
2 Wenn es schön ist, spiele ich Tennis.
3 Wenn es regnet, gehe ich zum Sportzentrum.

2b Schreib Sätze für die drei anderen Bilder.
Write sentences for the three other pictures.

dreiundsechzig **63**

8.2 Was machen wir?

Meine Freizeit

1 Wann und wo treffen sie sich? Schreib Sätze.
When and where are they meeting? Write sentences.

a. Wir treffen uns um sieben Uhr am Rathaus.

b. _____

c. _____

d. _____

e. _____

f. _____

2 Bring den Dialog in die richtige Reihenfolge.
Put the conversation in the correct order.

Hallo, Anna, hier Max. [1]

An der Post. [ ]

Okay, wir können dann auf die Eisbahn gehen. [ ]

Tschüs. [ ]

Um sieben Uhr. [ ]

Das Kino, eigentlich nicht. Der Film ist sehr langweilig. [ ]

Ja, tolle Idee. Wann treffen wir uns? [ ]

Gut, danke. Willst du morgen ins Kino gehen? [ ]

Und wo? [ ]

Hallo, Max. Wie geht's? [ ]

Prima, bis dann. [ ]

64 vierundsechzig

8.3 Im Supermarkt

Meine Freizeit

1 Wie viel Geld ist das? Finde die passenden Wörter.
How much? Match the prices to the right picture.

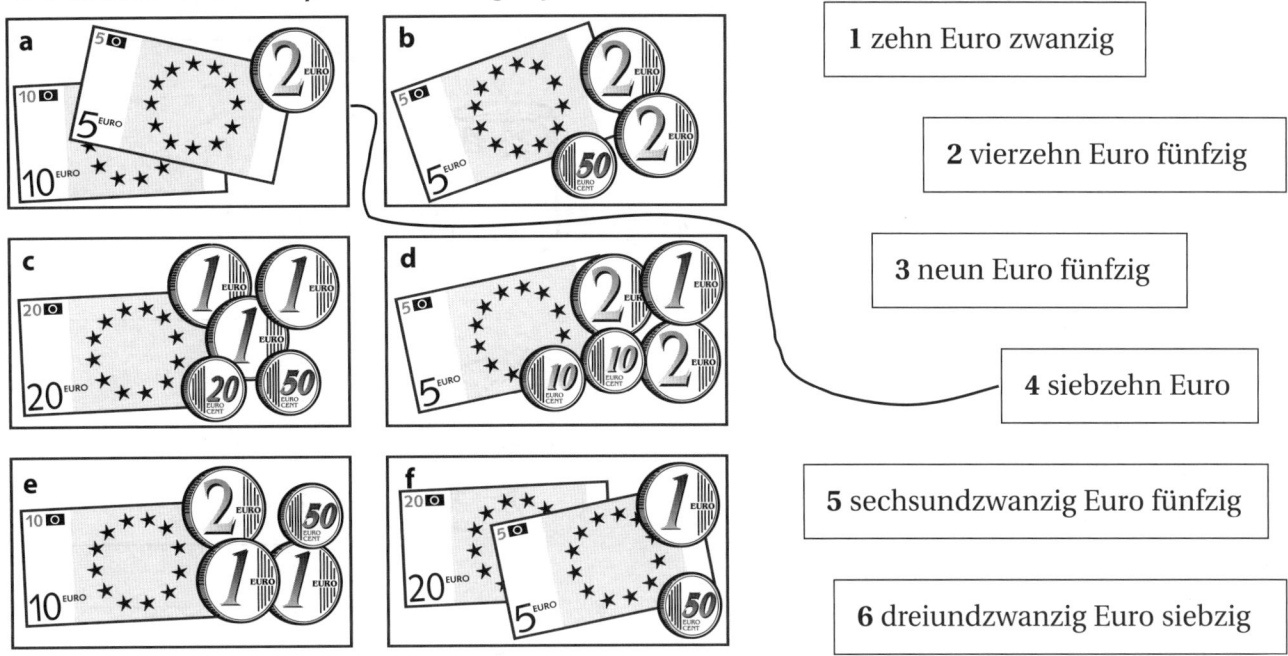

1 zehn Euro zwanzig

2 vierzehn Euro fünfzig

3 neun Euro fünfzig

4 siebzehn Euro

5 sechsundzwanzig Euro fünfzig

6 dreiundzwanzig Euro siebzig

2a Lies die Broschüre und schreib die Preise auf.
Read the brochure and write in the correct prices.

PRIMA Supermarkt

Limonade Flasche	€ 0,80	Kartoffelsalat 500 Gramm	€ 2,50
10 Brötchen	€ 3,00	Jogurt 8 Becher	€ 4,80
Kekse Packung	€ 1,90	Cola 6 Dosen	€ 6,60
Chips Tüte	€ 1,20	Orangensaft 1 Flasche	€ 1,50

2b Schreib den Kassenzettel zu Ende.
Complete the receipt.

a zwölf Dosen Cola = €13,20
b sechs Tüten Chips =
c zwei Kilo Kartoffelsalat =
d vier Becher Jogurt =
e neun Packungen Kekse =
f zwei Flaschen Limonade =
g fünf Flaschen Orangensaft =
h sieben Brötchen =

fünfundsechzig **65**

8.4 Im Café — Meine Freizeit

1) Was bestellen sie?
What are these people ordering? Fill in the speech bubbles.

a) Ich möchte eine Limonade, bitte.

b)

c)

d)

e)

f)

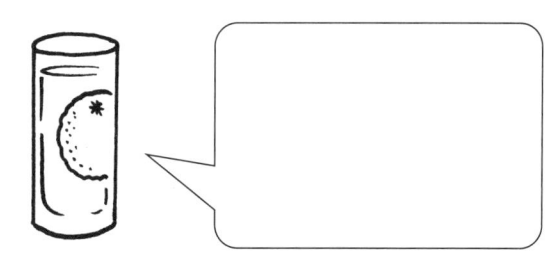

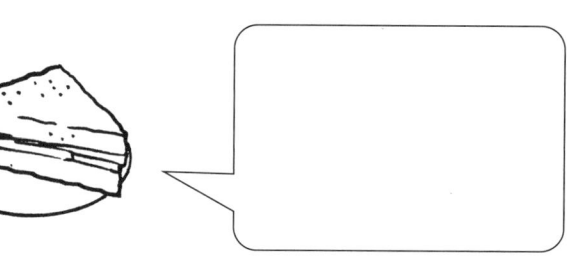

2) Lies die Gespräche und schau die Bilder an. Welches Gespräch ist das?
Read the conversations and look at the pictures. Which conversation is it, A or B?

A

Kellner: Guten Tag.
Kunde: Guten Tag. Ich möchte einen Kaffee und einen Apfelstrudel, bitte.
Kellner: Es tut mir Leid, wir haben keinen Apfelstrudel mehr.
Kunde: Dann nehme ich Schwarzwälder Kirschtorte.
Kellner: Gut, ist das alles?
Kunde: Ja. Vielen Dank.

B

Kellner: Guten Tag.
Kunde: Guten Tag. Ich möchte ein Käsebrot, bitte.
Kellner: Und zu trinken?
Kunde: Zu trinken nehme ich einen Orangensaft.
Kellner: Gut, ist das alles?
Kunde: Ich möchte auch ein Vanilleeis.
Kellner: Danke, kommt sofort.

a   b   c   d   e   f

8 Grammatik 1

Meine Freizeit

Flashback

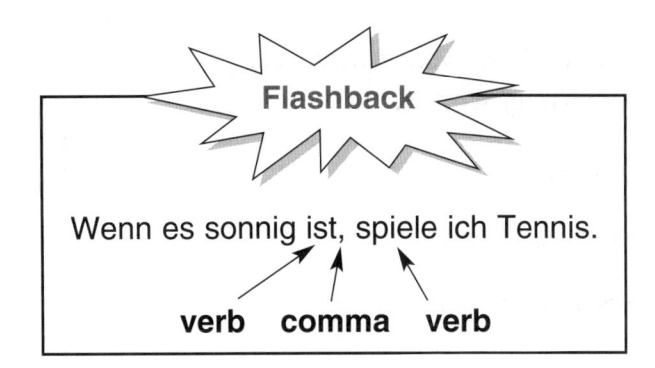

Wenn es sonnig ist, spiele ich Tennis.
  verb   comma   verb

1 Schreib die Sätze richtig auf.
Write the sentences in the correct order.

a Wenn | sonnig | , | gehe | schwimmen | ich | es | ist | .

_____

b Windsurfen | gehe | Wenn | es | , | windig | . | ist | ich

_____

c Kino | kalt | ist | , | es | . | Wenn | ins | ich | gehe

_____

d sonnig | Tennis | ich | spiele | Wenn | . | es | , | ist

_____

2 Was machen sie bei welchem Wetter? Schreib Sätze.
What do they do in what weather? Write sentences.

a Wenn es schneit, fahre ich Ski.

b _____

c _____

d _____

e _____

siebenundsechzig **67**

Grammatik 2

Meine Freizeit

1 Füll die Lücken mir der richtigen Form von *wollen* aus.
Fill the gaps with the correct form of wollen.

a Ich _____ ins Kino gehen.

b _____ du auf die Eisbahn gehen?

c Jana _____ einen Einkaufsbummel machen.

d Oliver und Daniel _____ schwimmen gehen.

e Was _____ ihr machen?

f Wir _____ ins Sportzentrum gehen.

g _____ Sie ins Museum gehen?

Flashback

wollen
ich will
du willst
er/sie/es will
wir wollen
ihr wollt
Sie wollen
sie wollen

2 Füll die Lücken mit der richtigen Form von *können* aus.
Fill the gaps with the correct form of können.

a Wir _____ ein Picknick machen.

b _____ du schwimmen? Ich _____ nicht schwimmen.

c _____ ihr Tennis spielen?

d Thomas _____ nicht Ski fahren.

e Anja und Ute _____ sehr gut Basketball spielen.

f _____ Sie Basketball spielen?

Flashback

können
ich kann
du kannst
er/sie/es kann
wir können
ihr könnt
Sie können
sie können

3 Welche Frage passt zu welcher Antwort?
Draw lines to match the questions and answers.

1 Was wollt ihr machen?
2 Was willst du machen?
3 Was wollt ihr essen?
4 Was willst du trinken?
5 Willst du Tennis spielen?
6 Was wollen Sie essen?
7 Was können wir in Stuttgart machen?

a Ich will eine Pizza essen.
b Nein, danke. Ich kann nicht Tennis spielen.
c Wir können ins Kino gehen.
d Wir wollen schwimmen gehen.
e Wir wollen Hamburger mit Pommes essen.
f Ich will auf die Eisbahn gehen.
g Ich will einen Orangensaft trinken.

68 *achtundsechzig*

Vokabular

Meine Freizeit

Wie ist das Wetter?

Es ist sonnig.
Es regnet.
Es ist schön.
Es ist heiß.
Es ist kalt.
Es ist frostig.
Es schneit.
Es gewittert.

Es ist neblig.
Es ist bewölkt.
Es ist warm.
Es ist windig.
Wenn es regnet, gehe ich zum Sportzentrum.

Was machen wir?

Ich will zum Park gehen.
Wir können ins Sportzentrum gehen.
Was willst du machen?
Wann und wo treffen wir uns?
Wir treffen uns um drei Uhr an der Post.

Im Supermarkt

Was darf es sein?
Was kostet das?
Das kostet …
   ein Euro vierzig
   zwei Euro achtzig
   sechzig Cent
ein Kilo
500 Gramm

What is the weather like?

It's sunny.
It's raining.
It's fine.
It's hot.
It's cold.
It's frosty.
It's snowing.
There's thunder and lightning.
It's foggy.
It's cloudy.
It's warm.
it's windy.

sports centre.

What shall we do?

I want to go to the park.
We can go to the sports centre.
What do you want to do?
When and where shall we meet?
Let's meet at 3 o'clock at the post office.

In the supermarket

What would you like?
What does that cost?
It costs …
   one euro forty
   two euros eighty
   60 cents
a kilo
500 grammes

eine Packung
eine Flasche
eine Dose
eine Tüte
ein Becher
ein Liter
Milch
Käse
Orangensaft
Marmelade
Eier
Limonade
Mineralwasser
Jogurt
Kekse
Kartoffelsalat
Schinken
Orangen

Im Café

Ich nehme …
   ein Käsebrot
   einen Hamburger mit Pommes
   eine Pizza mit Salat
   Apfelstrudel
   Schwarzwälder Kirschtorte
   Pflaumenkuchen
   ein Vanilleeis
   ein Schokoladeneis
   ein Erdbeereis
   eine Cola
   einen Tee
   einen Kaffee
   eine heiße Schokolade mit Sahne

a packet
a bottle
a can
a bag
a tub
a litre
milk
cheese
orange juice
jam
eggs
lemonade
mineral water
yoghurt
biscuits
potato salad
ham
oranges

In the café

I'll have …
   a cheese sandwich
   a hamburger with chips
   a pizza with salad
   apple strudel
   Black Forest gateau

   plum cake
   a vanilla ice cream
   a chocolate ice cream
   a strawberry ice cream
   a cola
   a tea
   a coffee
   a hot chocolate with cream

neunundsechzig

8 Kannst du …? Checklist

Meine Freizeit

This is a checklist of the things you should aim to learn in German using Klasse! neu 1. *Use the* **Check** *boxes and the* **Prove it!** *column to keep track of what you have learned.*

★ Tick the first box when you feel you are getting to grips with the learning objective, but sometimes need a prompt or time to think.

★ Tick the second box when you think you have fully mastered the learning objective and will be able to use it again in future.

★ Make notes following the prompts in the **Prove it!** column to help you show what you have learned. Your learning partner or parent can test you and initial the second box to confirm the progress you have made.

Learning objectives	Check		Prove it!
I can ask what the weather is like.	☐	☐	*Get partner to test you.*
I can describe the weather.	☐	☐	*Get partner to test you.*
I can say what I do depending on the weather.	☐	☐	*Get partner to test you.*
I can use the correct word order after *wenn*.	☐	☐	*Get partner to test you.*
I can make plans for going out.	☐	☐	*Get partner to test you.*
I can ask what somebody wants to do.	☐	☐	*Get partner to test you.*
I can arrange to meet.	☐	☐	*Get partner to test you.*
I can use modal verbs *können* and *wollen*.	☐	☐	*Get partner to test you.*
I can talk about German money.	☐	☐	*Get partner to test you.*
I can ask and say how much something costs.	☐	☐	*Get partner to test you.*
I can say what I want to buy.	☐	☐	*Get partner to test you.*
I can order food and drink in a café.	☐	☐	*Get partner to test you.*
I can use more polite language.	☐	☐	*Get partner to test you.*

9.1 Heute Abend fahre ich in die Stadt!

Ein Wochenende in Hollfeld

1 Füll die Lücken aus.
Fill in the gaps.

a zu_ H_l_ _nb_ _
b zu_ Sp_r_z_ _t_um 
c z_ _ Sc_ _l_ 
d z_ _ K_ _o 
e z_r D_ _c_ 
f zu_ P_ _k 

2 Füll die Lücken aus.
Fill in the gaps.

| 10 Uhr | dem Rad | Markt |
| Nachmittag | Vati | Post |

a Ich fahre am Samstag mit _____ zum Supermarkt.
b Ich gehe am _____ zu Fuß zum Schwimmbad.
c Wir fahren am Morgen mit dem Bus zum _____ .
d Ich fahre mit _____ mit dem Zug in die Stadt.
e Wir gehen heute Morgen zu Fuß zur _____ .
f Wir fahren am Wochenende um _____ zum Park.

3 Was machst du am Wochenende? Schreib einen Brief.
Write a letter to your penfriend with the information below.

| Ich | fahre / gehe | am Freitag / am Samstag / am Sonntag / am Wochenende | | |

einundsiebzig 71

9.2 Was machst du am Wochenende?

Ein Wochenende in Hollfeld

1 Wie heißt das auf Englisch?
Translate the German sentences into English. Make sure you use the correct tense.

a Ich spiele Tennis. _____

b Ich habe im Internet gesurft. _____

c Ich habe Pizza gemacht. _____

d Ich höre Musik. _____

e Ich mache Sport. _____

f Ich habe gekocht. _____

2 Schreib die passenden Wörter auf.
Find the correct words.

a Ich habe Salat _____ .

b Ich habe im Internet _____ .

c Ich habe Mittagessen _____ .

d Ich habe Musik _____ .

e Ich habe Sport _____ .

f Ich habe einen Auflauf _____ .

| gemacht | gekocht | gehört | gesurft | gemacht | gekocht |

3 Du bist dran – schreib Sätze.
Write sentences.

Beispiel: Am Montag habe ich Fußball gespielt.

| Montag | Dienstag | Mittwoch | Donnerstag | Freitag | Samstag | Sonntag |

72 zweiundsiebzig

9.3 Was hast du am Samstag gemacht?

Ein Wochenende in Hollfeld

1 Was hat Jens am Wochenende gemacht? Füll die Lücken aus.
What did Jens do at the weekend? Fill in the gaps.

Freitagabend

Samstag

Samstagabend

Sonntag

Sonntagabend

Liebe Ulla,

was hast du am Wochenende gemacht?

Also, Freitagabend: Ich _habe Hausaufgaben gemacht_____ .

Am Samstag? Ich _____ .

Und ich _____ !

Und abends? Ich _____ .

Ich habe am Sonntag viel gemacht: Ich _____

_____ und ich _____

_____ . Und am Abend?

Ich _____ .

Ach ja, und ich _____ .

Tschüs!

Jens

dreiundsiebzig **73**

9.4 Sonntag im Park — Ein Wochenende in Hollfeld

1 Sonntag im Park: Was haben sie gemacht? Schreib Sätze.
What did they do in the park on Sunday? Write sentences.

1 Wir haben _____.
2 Wir sind _____.
3 Wir haben _____.
4 Wir sind _____.
5 Wir haben _____.
6 Wir sind _____
   _____.
7 Wir haben _____.

74 vierundsiebzig

Grammatik 1

Ein Wochenende in Hollfeld

Flashback

			haben		**past participle**
Ich tanze in der Disco.	→	Ich	habe	in der Disco	getanzt.
Du hörst Musik.	→	Du	hast	Musik	gehört.
Wir kaufen CDs.	→	Wir	haben	CDs	gekauft.

!

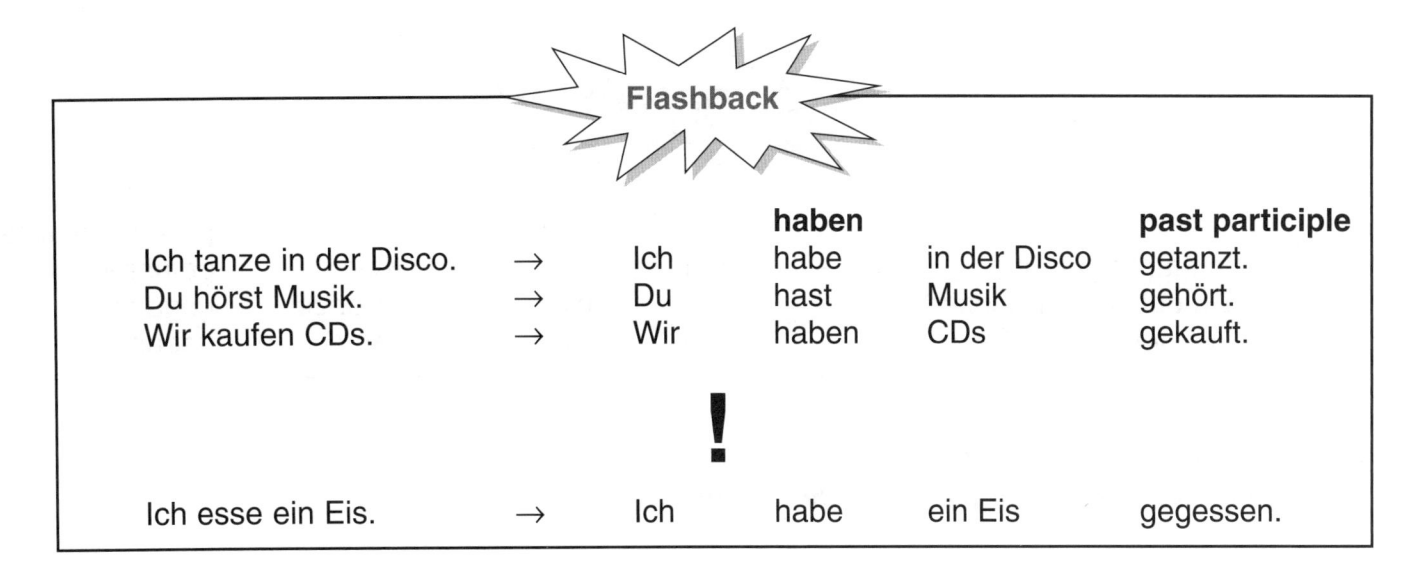

| Ich esse ein Eis. | → | Ich | habe | ein Eis | gegessen. |

1 Füll die Lücken aus.
Fill in the gaps.

- **a** Ich habe ein Eis _____ .
- **b** Wir haben in der Disco _____ .
- **c** Ich habe Pizza mit Spinat _____ .
- **d** Wir haben eine CD _____ .
- **e** Ich habe Basketball _____ .
- **f** Wir haben Musik _____ .

2 Schreib die Sätze im Perfekt auf.
Write the sentences in the perfect tense.

- **a** Wir spielen Tennis. _____
- **b** Ich kaufe eine Cola. _____
- **c** Wir machen Nudelsalat. _____
- **d** Wir tanzen in der Disco. _____
- **e** Ich höre Musik. _____
- **f** Wir essen Pommes frites. _____

fünfundsiebzig **75**

Grammatik 2

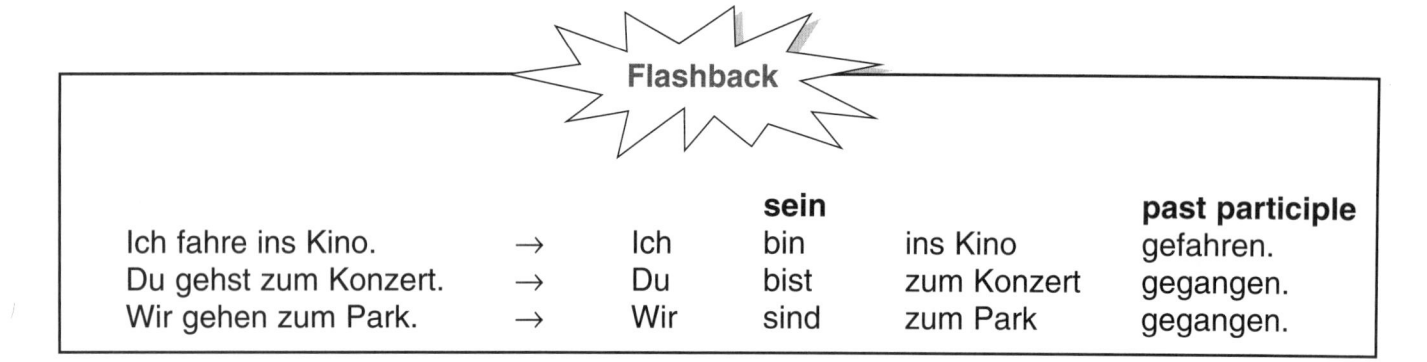

Ein Wochenende in Hollfeld

Flashback

			sein		**past participle**
Ich fahre ins Kino.	→	Ich	bin	ins Kino	gefahren.
Du gehst zum Konzert.	→	Du	bist	zum Konzert	gegangen.
Wir gehen zum Park.	→	Wir	sind	zum Park	gegangen.

1 Finde die passenden Bilder.
Draw lines to match the pictures to the sentences.

a Ich bin Rollschuh gefahren.

b Wir sind ins Kino gegangen.

c Ich bin zum Sportzentrum gefahren.

d Ich bin zum Park gegangen.

e Wir sind Skateboard gefahren.

f Wir sind zum Konzert gegangen.

2 *sein* oder *haben*? Füll die Lücken aus.
Fill in the gaps with the correct forms of sein *or* haben.

a Wir _____ zur Schule gefahren.

b Ich _____ Volleyball gespielt.

c Wir _____ einen Spaziergang gemacht.

d Ich _____ in die Stadt gegangen.

e Wir _____ zum Park gefahren.

f Ich _____ ein Erdbeereis gegessen.

76 sechsundsiebzig

Vokabular

Ein Wochenende in Hollfeld

Was hast du letzten Samstag/gestern gemacht?

Ich habe ...
- (Mittagessen) gekocht.
- Pizza/Pommes frites mit Würstchen gemacht.
- Musik gehört.
- im Internet gesurft.
- einen Quiz/Sport/Surfboarding gemacht.

Was hast du am Wochenende gemacht?

Ich habe ...
Wir haben ...
- Fußball/Tennis/Karten gespielt.

What did you do last Saturday/yesterday?

I ...
- cooked (lunch).
- made pizza/chips with sausages.
- listened to music.
- surfed the internet.
- did a quiz/sports/surfboarding.

What did you do at the weekend?

I ...
We ...
- played football/tennis/cards.

- Souvenirs/CDs gekauft.
- in der Disco getanzt.
- Mittagessen gemacht.
- Pizza gegessen.

Sonntag im Park

Ich bin .../Wir sind ...
- zum Park/Skateboard gefahren.
- ins Kino/zum Konzert gegangen.

Ich habe .../Wir haben ...
- ein Picknick/einen Spaziergang gemacht.
- Kakao und Cola getrunken.
- eine Band gehört.

- bought souvenirs/CDs.
- danced in the disco.
- made lunch.
- ate pizza.

Sunday in the park

I .../We ...
- went to the park/did skateboarding.
- went to the cinema/concert.

I .../We ...
- had a picnic/went for a walk.
- drank hot chocolate and coke.
- listened to a band.

9 Kannst du …? Checklist

Ein Wochenende in Hollfeld

This is a checklist of the things you should aim to learn in German using Klasse! neu 1. *Use the* **Check** *boxes and the* **Prove it!** *column to keep track of what you have learned.*

★ Tick the first box when you feel you are getting to grips with the learning objective, but sometimes need a prompt or time to think.

★ Tick the second box when you think you have fully mastered the learning objective and will be able to use it again in future.

★ Make notes following the prompts in the **Prove it!** column to help you show what you have learned. Your learning partner or parent can test you and initial the second box to confirm the progress you have made.

Learning objectives	Check		Prove it!
I can describe what I do at the weekend.	☐	☐	*Get partner to test you.*
I can ask what someone did at the weekend.	☐	☐	*Get partner to test you.*
I can say what I did last weekend.	☐	☐	*Get partner to test you.*
I can talk about where I went last weekend.	☐	☐	*Get partner to test you.*
I can compare actions in the present and the past.	☐	☐	*Get partner to test you.*
I can recognize and use the perfect tense with *haben*.	☐	☐	*Get partner to test you.*
I can recognize and use the past tense with *sein*.	☐	☐	*Get partner to test you.*
I can use words to add detail.	☐	☐	*Get partner to test you.*
I can use the correct word order – TIME – MANNER – PLACE.	☐	☐	*Get partner to test you.*

Meine neuen Wörter

Klasse! neu 1 is the first stage of a revised edition of the popular course. Designed to provide a clear, fully-supported and flexible approach to teaching the Modern Languages Framework, this new edition should appeal to all learners.

Klasse! neu 1 *Extra!* Workbook complements the Students' Book, providing additional support and language practice. It is ideal for homework and independent classroom study.

This workbook provides:
- extra practice material for the key language and Framework objectives launched in each unit
- pages to consolidate key grammar points
- a vocabulary list for each unit
- unit checklists, for pupils to record their own progress.

Students' Book 1
Noch mal! 1 Workbook
Extra! 1 Workbook
Teacher's Book 1
Copymaster Book 1
Set of CDs 1
Set of cassettes 1
OHT File 1
Flashcards (Parts 1–2)*
Coursemaster CD-ROM
Klasse! neu 1 Integral Teacher's edition
Klasse! neu 1 Integral Students' edition
as per original set

OXFORD UNIVERSITY PRESS

www.OxfordSecondary.co.uk

Orders and enquiries to Customer Services:
tel. 01536 452620   fax 01865 313472
schools.enquiries.uk@oup.com

ISBN 978-0-19-840647-1

9 780198 406471